Winning Meetings and Events for your Venue

Winning Meetings and Events for your Venue

Rob Davidson and Anthony Hyde

(G) **Goodfellow Publishers Ltd**

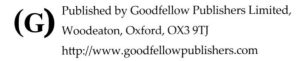 Published by Goodfellow Publishers Limited,
Woodeaton, Oxford, OX3 9TJ

http://www.goodfellowpublishers.com

 Design and typesetting by P.K. McBride, www.macbride.org.uk

Printed by Marston Book Services, www.marston.co.uk

Cover design by Cylinder

Contents

Preface

Although, at first sight, we may appear to come from dissimilar professional backgrounds – Anthony as a practitioner in venue management, sales and operations; and Rob as an educator and trainer specialising in conference management – we both share a strong conviction that venues of all types play a powerful role in today's meetings industry. Venues from conference centres and hotels to 'unusual', non-traditional venues can considerably enhance the experience of those who attend the meetings and events that they host, and can play a key part in helping those meetings and events achieve their various goals and objectives.

The past few decades have seen far-reaching changes in both the quality and quantity of the venues operating in the meetings industry. On the one hand, we have witnessed vast advances in the ways in which venues are designed and constructed, resulting in more flexible, ergonomic meeting spaces that can easily adapt to changing meetings trends and enrich the experience of attendees. On the other, we have seen a considerable expansion in the supply of new venues offering facilities for meetings and events. Part of this expansion has come as a result of the growing number of new destinations targeting the market for meetings and events, particularly in regions such as South-East Asia and the Middle East, where the recent increase in the supply of conference centres and hotels with meetings facilities has been phenomenal. But part of this expansion has also resulted from the rapid growth in non-traditional venues, generated by facilities such as museums, theatres and tourist attractions increasingly targeting meetings and events as a secondary source of income.

However, while changes in the physical product of venues have been widely acknowledged, we believe that insufficient attention has been paid to the skills and knowledge of those people who are employed by venues to identify potential buyers and persuade them to hold their meetings in their facility. Every venue has at least one employee with responsibility for winning business; and larger venues may have an entire team of colleagues engaging in sales and marketing activities. Their job titles vary widely, but Sales and Marketing Manager, Conference and Banqueting Manager and Events Manager are some of those most commonly used in the English-speaking world.

It is clear that any venue's success in the meetings sector depends directly upon the effectiveness of these employees in winning meetings, conferences and other events. For, although demand for face-to-face meetings is expanding in all world regions, the supply of venues has outstripped this expansion, leading to a fiercely competitive market situation.

Against this background of intense competition between venues, we have identified a major challenge: a significant proportion of those with responsibility for selling meetings facilities in their venues are poorly prepared for this task, largely due to the distinct lack of any easily accessible source of information on the techniques and tools necessary to do this work in an effective manner and bring the best possible results. The effect is that very many of those charged with filling the meetings spaces of their venues with events are under-performing through their lack of awareness of the best sales and marketing practices. This can result in widespread lost opportunities for winning business – and therefore lost revenue for the venue, a lack of job satisfaction for those in venue sales and marketing posts, and consequent high turnover among such employees.

This book represents a key step towards filling this commonly-found gap in knowledge and expertise. It has been written to respond to the demands of two principal categories of readers. First, those already employed in sales and marketing positions in venues of all types will find in the book a clear and comprehensive guide to ideas and techniques that will enable them to expand their existing knowledge of how to win business for their venues. Second, the book's content will be welcomed by today's fast-growing body of students of hospitality, tourism and events management, for whom a career in venue sales and marketing is an attractive vocation. The content of this book will prepare them for successful employment in sales positions in any type of venue currently targeting the market for meetings and events.

In *Winning Meetings and Events for your Venue*, we have combined our extensive experience and up-to-date knowledge of venue sales techniques and the meetings and events market with examples of best-practice from venues around the world to produce a book that we are confident will be a source of new ideas and useful, practical techniques to anyone already working in venue sales or planning to do so in the near future.

Rob Davidson and Anthony Hyde. January 2014.

About the authors

Rob Davidson is a Senior Lecturer at the University of Greenwich where he teaches Events Management, focusing on business events. His principal area of expertise is the conference and incentive travel sector, and he writes widely on this subject. He regularly contributes articles to the professional business tourism press, including Conference News, in which he writes a monthly column. In addition, he runs his own consultancy, and has undertaken research for many high-profile MICE organisations.

Each year, at the EIBTM trade show in Barcelona, he launches his annual Trendswatch report on trends in the conference and incentive industry. On five occasions, he has been included in *Conference & Incentive Travel* magazine's 'Power 50' – the 50 most influential people in the UK conference industry.

Anthony Hyde is a specialist in venue management, sales and operations. Formerly General Manager of the Business Events division at the Barbican, one of Europe's largest combined arts and conference centres, Anthony was responsible for sales, marketing, public relations, management and technical production for conferences, banqueting, exhibitions and corporate hospitality. He focussed the Business Events strategy on content and the objectives that underpin meetings and events. He has steered the business successfully through a difficult economic period, while continually developing the product, launching a new venue at the Guildhall School of Music and Drama, and capitalising on the success of the Olympics.

Anthony is past president of Meeting Professionals International (MPI) UK and Ireland Chapter and remains an active member. He also sits on the boards of the Association of British Professional Conference Organisers (ABPCO) and the London City Selection, a consortium of venues within the City of London which he also co-founded.

Anthony now works with clients internationally on all aspects of venue management, including strategic direction, business planning, design and operations.

1 The Structure of the Meetings and Events Industry

This chapter covers:

- The value of meetings
- Meetings terminology
- Classification of meetings
- Segmentation of demand for meetings

Meetings of all kinds – from international conferences and summits for several thousand delegates to board meetings, training seminars and team-building events for smaller groups of colleagues – are playing an increasingly important role in the business, intellectual, political and cultural life of communities worldwide. Demand for meetings comes from a wide variety of sources including all types of businesses, governments, academics, and the vast range of associations, clubs, federations and interest groups that bring together people with a common interest, from a shared profession to a hobby/sport/leisure pursuit enjoyed by the members.

In order to meet this escalating demand for such gatherings, there has been considerable investment in meetings facilities in all regions of the world over recent years. Cities and resorts worldwide have spent vast sums of money constructing purpose-built conference centres or renovating existing facilities. The global hotel industry has also recognised the importance to its profitability of hosting and servicing meetings, and has expanded its offer in this area; and an increasing number of residential conference centres are available in universities and colleges. There is also a rapidly increasing number of 'unusual venues' being promoted as places where meetings may be held. Unusual venues are based in establishments that have a primary function that is not directly linked to the hospitality/meetings industry. These include cultural venues (museums, cinemas, theatres, etc.), sports venues (football stadia, racecourses, cricket grounds, etc) and tourist attractions such as historic monuments, castles, zoos and aquaria, and theme parks). In *The Future of Booking Venues* by Eades and Brewerton for the UK's Hotel Booking Agency Association, Tim Chudley, Managing Director of the Sundial Group of venues is quoted as saying:

> The past 10 years as a period of time has seen most notably the massive increase in supply. It does seem now that every type of location is hoping to tap into the meetings and conferences market as a secondary revenue stream. Competition can now be found in the form of stadia, museums, tourist attractions and, in one village close to one of our properties, the village shop promoting 'meeting rooms'.

Venues of all types play a vital role in the hosting of the great variety of meetings and events that take place in destinations worldwide, and this makes them key stakeholders in the meetings industry. This chapter examines the structure of the industry, but begins with a review of the value of meetings to the destinations and venues that host them and to the people who initiate them and attend them.

The value of meetings

The different types of value arising from the hosting of meetings and events may be divided into two categories: the tourism-related benefits and the non-tourism related benefits.

■ Tourism benefits

In terms of the tourism benefits, those attending meetings fill hotel bedrooms, seats on aircraft and other forms of transport, and places at restaurant tables; and their spending can extend into local shops as well as entertainment and leisure facilities. More than that, travel for the purpose of attending meetings often represents the high-quality, high-yield end of the tourism spectrum, with corporate meetings in particular creating demand for premium seats on trains and planes, and the higher categories of hotel accommodation.

In addition, meetings attendance is generally an all-year-round activity even if demand tends to dip in the summer months. In this sense, the seasonality pattern for meetings-related travel complements that of leisure-related tourism, which for many destinations and hospitality businesses peaks in the summer months. Moreover, meetings tend to be scheduled during the working week, again providing complementarity with the leisure market, which generally focuses on weekends.

Finally, the tourism industry benefits from meetings whenever participants in such events take one or more of these actions:

☐ Come accompanied by family members or friends who make use of the tourism attractions of the destination

☐ Extend their business trip for leisure-related purposes, by arriving some days before the meeting and/or staying on a few days after the meeting, in effect turning the trip into a holiday

☐ Return to the meetings destination, with friends or family, for leisure purposes, motivated by the experience of their trip to the same destination in order to attend a meeting.

■ Non-tourism benefits

The non-tourism related benefits take the following forms:

☐ Many cities have invested in meetings facilities, such as flagship conference centres, as an element of plans to regenerate urban areas in need of re-development. From Glasgow and Philadelphia to Cape Town and Dublin, large-scale meetings facilities have been built as a means of bringing prosperity and animation back into previously neglected parts of those cities.

☐ More intangibly, the fact of hosting a conference, in particular an international event, can be a source of pride and prestige for the city or country where the conference takes place, as well as a means of creating an image or brand for itself, in the international community of nations.

Tony Rogers makes the point well in his book, *Conferences and Conventions:* 'There is undoubted prestige in being selected to host a major international conference, and some less developed countries would see this as a way of gaining credibility and acceptance on the international political stage'. For example, there can be little doubt that national pride and image-building were factors behind Yugoslavia (as it then still was) offering to host the 1979 International Monetary Fund conference, and building a new venue, the Sava Centar in Belgrade, specifically for that event.

In a 2009 briefing paper released by the global peak body of the meetings industry, the Joint Meetings Industry Council, entitled 'Key Messages for the Meetings Industry', a wide range of benefits derived from business events were identified. Apart from the more obvious economic impacts generated as a result of delegate expenditure, the benefits listed in this paper that "are critical to the business, scientific, professional, educational and cultural life and development of a community" were:

☐ Meetings attract investment by attracting an often influential audience of participants, and creating opportunities for showcasing local products, services, and investment opportunities.

☐ Meetings enhance professional development by bringing regional and international expertise into the community, where it is accessible to local professionals.

☐ Meetings enhance science and technology, which helps generate new forms of technology itself, improves understanding and access to it, and helps improve local knowledge and skills by bringing outside information and technology into the host community and providing a vehicle for local businesses and professionals to access the latest developments in their respective fields.

☐ Meetings promote cultural exchange by providing new forums for cultural exchange and new opportunities to expose local culture to national and international audiences.

Elaborating upon the third of the JMIC impacts listed above, Jago and Deery, in their publication, *Delivering Innovation, Knowledge and Performance: The Role of Business Events*, focused on the potential of meetings and events to be a key tool in the knowledge creation and dissemination processes that are so fundamental to improving business performance and underpinning innovation. They acknowledged that that such impacts are longer-term and more difficult to quantify than tourism benefits, but they make a convincing case that meetings can bring many beneficial outcomes leading to the creation and dissemination of innovative practices and the enhancement of individual and organisational performance. Figure 1.1 represents their analysis of the range of outcomes from meetings and events.

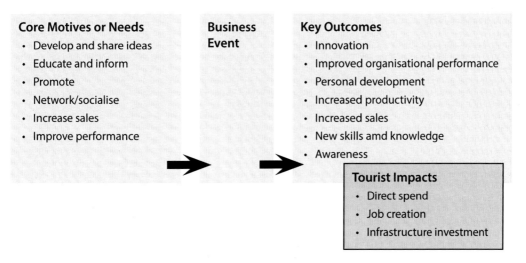

Figure 1.1: Key motives and outcomes for meetings and events. Source: Jago L and Deery M (2010) *Delivering Innovation, Knowledge and Performance: The Role of Business Events*

Terminology

Any analysis of the structure of the meetings industry inevitably encounters problems of terminology. Despite the rapid growth of the meetings industry – or perhaps, because of that rapid growth, there is a lack of standardised terminology that is universally accepted. Even the meetings industry bodies differ in the definitions they use, leading to frequent confusion, particularly when international comparisons of meetings industry data are attempted. Many terms are used interchangeably and even within the English language terms for meetings-related concepts, there are differences between how those concepts are labelled in North American English and English as used in Europe.

For the industry as a whole, several terms are used to differing degrees:

☐ **Business tourism**. This expression is well-established but only in certain circles. Problems with this term can arise, for example, due to the fact that the link with tourism can be tenuous for some categories of meetings where very little actual travel takes place – a corporate meeting held in a local hotel, for example. The term is hardly ever used in North American English, where 'business' and 'tourism' are contrasting terms and to combine them would amount to an oxymoron.

☐ **MICE** is an acronym, for Meetings, Incentives, Conferences, Exhibitions (IAPCO Online Dictionary). Its appeal as a shorthand expression is widespread. However, the main problem with this term is that practically no-one outside the industry understands what it means, not least the politicians whose support is so vital to the industry's growth. It is a convenient 'in-joke' lacking general recognition.

☐ **The Meetings industry**. Recently, there has been an industry-driven initiative, led by the International Congress and Convention Association (ICCA), Meeting Professionals International (MPI) and Reed Travel against the use of the MICE label and in support of using the Meetings industry as an alternative. The initiative's success has been hindered by the fact that MICE appears to be the preferred term precisely in countries in those world regions such as the Middle East and South East Asia, where the industry is expanding considerably.

☐ **Business events** is an alternative term that has been adopted more recently in some major markets such as Australia and Canada, based on the fact that meetings have much in common with other types of events (cultural, sports, for example) in the sense that they are planned, temporary occasions taking place in venues and aimed at a specific, invited, audience. The Business Events Council of Australia defines a business event as: 'Any public or private activity consisting of a minimum of 15 persons with a common interest or vocation, held in a specific venue or venues, and hosted by an organisation (or organisations). This may include (but not limited to): conferences, conventions, symposia, congresses, incentive group events, marketing events, special celebrations, seminars, courses, public or trade shows, product launches, exhibitions, company annual general meetings, corporate retreats, study tours or training programs'.

■ Classification of meetings by type

Ongoing problems of terminology are also encountered at the level of defining different types of meeting. While universal agreement on such definitions still evades the industry, one of the most detailed and widely recognised systems of classification is that used by the Convention Industry Council, as shown in Figure 1.2.

Conferences/ Conventions/ Congresses	A general term covering all non business-oriented gatherings of participants at a predetermined site and time to attend an organized meeting in which they have an interactive, debating, seminar, and/or competitive role, and of which the theme or purpose may be of any nature. These are hosted by professional, trade, or other non-corporate organisations. (See also specific definitions below).
Conference	1) Participatory meeting designed for discussion, fact-finding, problem solving and consultation. 2) An event used by any organization to meet and exchange views, convey a message, open a debate or give publicity to some area of opinion on a specific issue. No tradition, continuity, or periodicity is required to convene a conference. Although not generally limited in time, conferences are usually of short duration with specific objectives. Conferences are generally on a smaller scale than congresses.
Convention	1) A general and formal meeting of a legislative body, social, or economic group in order to provide information, deliberate or establish consent or policies among participants. In the United States, the term is used to describe large, usually national meetings of business circles, for discussion and/or commercial exhibition. 2) An event where the primary activity is to attend educational sessions, participate in meetings/discussions, socialise, or attend other organised events. There is a secondary exhibition component.
Congress	1) The regular coming together of large groups of individuals, generally to discuss a particular subject. A congress will often last several days and have several simultaneous sessions. The length of time between congresses is usually established in advance of the implementation stage and may be pluri-annual or annual. Most international or world congresses are of the former type while national congresses are more frequently held annually. 2) Meeting of an association of delegates or representatives from constituent organizations. 3) European term for convention.
Seminar	1) Lecture and dialogue allowing participants to share experiences in a particular field under the guidance of an expert discussion leader. 2) A meeting or series of meetings from 10 to 50 specialists who have different specific skills but have a common interest and come together for learning purposes. The work schedule of a seminar has the specific objective of enriching the skills of the participants.

Trade show/ business exhibition	1) An exhibition of products and/or services held for members of a common industry. The primary activity of attendees is visiting exhibits on the show floor. These events focus primarily on business-to-business relationships, but part of the event may be open to the general public. 2) Display of products or promotional material for the purpose of public relations, sales and/or marketing.
Incentive event	A reward event intended to showcase persons who meet or exceed sales or production goals.
Corporate/ business meeting	1) Business-oriented meeting usually hosted by a corporation, in which participants represent the same company, corporate group or client/provider relationships. 2) Gathering of employees or representatives of a commercial organisation Usually, attendance is required and most expenses are paid for by the organisation.

Figure 1.2: CIC Categorisation of Meetings. Adapted from Convention Industry Council (2011) *The Economic Significance of Meetings to the US Economy.*

■   Classification by objectives

The CIC system of classification gives some indication, in places, of the purposes behind the different types of meeting. But Adrian Segar, in his publication, *Conferences that work: Creating Events That People Love*, comprehensively classifies conferences according to the objectives of those who attend them and initiate them. He considers the principal objectives to be as follows. Several are self-explanatory, but clarifications are included for those that are less so:

1   **Acquiring knowledge and getting answers**

2   **Conferring with other delegates**

3   **Meeting and connecting with peers**

4   **Establishing and increasing professional status**

Some conferences have a reputation for being must-attend events for those seeking to rise to the top of the associated profession or business. Presenters and panellists gain status, of course, simply from being chosen as presenters and panellists. But conferences also provide delegates with multiple opportunities for overtly promoting, adjusting, and reinforcing their professional status in discussions with presenters and fellow-attendees.

5   **Maintaining professional certification**

Many conferences exist for the sole purpose of maintaining professional certification. Continuing Education Units (CEUs), required to

maintain professional licensure, are awarded at about 100,000 conferences each year in the United States alone. (For many licensed professionals, these events are the only kind of conference they attend). Few
would argue against the regulation of professions requiring a high level
of specialized skill, and continuing professional development opportunities help refresh and update such skills.

6   Conferring legitimacy

When a new profession, field of study, or specialty begins emerging,
one of the first signs is the organising of a related conference. Interestingly,
such initial conferences are generally small, informally organised, and
exciting for the participants. Because they usually predate printed works
on a subject, such as books, journals, and periodicals, such conferences
are a principal way in which their subject becomes legitimised as worthy
of existing in its own right.

7   Issue activism

Examples of issue activism conferences are events that focus attention
on a political or social issue, incentive and morale boosting conferences
for sales people, and organisation or business planning events. What
these conferences have in common is an emphasis on creating change
around an issue; learning and sharing, though necessary, are usually
secondary concerns. Some organisers tightly script issue activism conferences to achieve a desired result. Only those who have bought into
the dominant conference viewpoint are likely to enjoy such events.

8   Building community

Some conferences are primarily about building community — finding
new ways to work with others — rather than exploring a particular topic.
(The approach to leadership known as the Art of Hosting exemplifies
this approach by putting conversation and participation at the centre of
their meetings, and employing appropriate processes to maximize and
harmonize meaningful human involvement. Other conference designs
recognize the importance of building community simultaneously as
attendees work together on solving community specific or organization problems. Formats such as Future Search, which helps a group of
people discover common ground and decide on appropriate responses,
and World Café, which supports small and large group dialogue around
central questions, use this approach).

Interestingly, Segar questions the ability of traditionally-designed conferences to deliver certain types of important learning experiences to attendees, and this issue will be examined in Chapter 7 of this book.

Demand for meetings

Sources of demand for meetings and events are wide-ranging and varied, and the next section of this chapter examines how the overall market can be segmented into its constituent parts. However, there are some characteristics common to all segments of demand.

For many years, this has been a buyers' market in most world regions, as the supply of new venues, combined with faltering national economies in many countries has often meant that supply of meetings facilities has outstripped demand. This market environment has put much of the power in negotiations in the hands of meeting planners and others responsible for selecting venues for their meetings and events. These stakeholders have become more demanding, as a result. And the growing professionalization of the meetings industry as a whole has meant that meeting planners are increasingly selecting venues on a strategic basis.

Minton (2005) describes how meetings planners are increasingly choosing conference centres on the basis of which venues makes the most strategic sense for their events: 'For planners, it's not what meetings they can bring to convention centres, but what those centres can bring to their meetings'. In other words, they are increasingly expecting venues not only to accommodate their events, but also to enhance them.

One aspect of the move towards the strategic booking of venues is that, in the decision-making process, a growing number of buyers are taking into account the extent to which venues reinforce their organisation's brand. One contributor to the HBAA publication, *The Future of Booking Venues*, explains that brands are precious to organisations because they can deliver a preference for their products or services, thus increasing sales; they can help attract the best employees; and they can build the value of the company. The contributor continues: 'Carrying your brand through meetings, events and venues creates a seamless continuation of your marketing strategy … The wrong choice of venue (for example,

1

contemporary brands and castles are not a natural 'fit'), theme and even meeting type can create a confused and rudderless message. Make sure your products are not compromised by competitor brands or advertising at the venue'.

Segmentation of demand for meetings

The most widely accepted classification of the different sectors of demand are corporate meetings, association meetings, government meetings and SMERF (Social Military, Educational, Religious and Fraternal) events. Each market segment has its own distinguishing characteristics, as described below. And venues' sales and marketing strategies must take those distinguishing features into account and adapt to each particular segment targeted.

■ ## Corporate meetings

Corporate meetings may be defined as gatherings of employees of commercial organisations. Usually attendance is required, and travel, accommodation and catering expenses are paid by the employer organisation.

Companies large and small have a number of reasons for organising meetings, but all are in some way linked to their need to operate effectively in the field of business.

Two types of corporate meeting may be identified:

☐   **Internal meetings** – for employees: For example, meetings held for the purpose of training staff in the skills and techniques that they need in order to perform well in the workplace – selling skills, customer relations skills, information technology skills and so on, depending on the nature of the company's business.

Other types of corporate meetings may be arranged with the objective of giving managers the opportunity to discuss the company's future strategies – for marketing, expansion, crisis management and so on. Most such meetings are comparatively small (ranging from a handful of employees to several dozen) and last one or two days on average.

☐   **External meetings** – for other stakeholders of the company: For example, shareholders' meetings, product presentations, press conferences – where those attending are not direct employees of the company.

■   Corporate events by objectives

An alternative method of classifying corporate events is to categorize them according to the primary objective for which the event is being held. Accordingly, the three principal categories are:

☐   **Legal/constitutional**: Internal or external meetings held for the purpose of, for instance, electing company directors or voting on business strategies.

☐   **Commercial**: Events designed directly to boost sales of the company's products or services. For example, new product presentations to clients or potential clients; or training sessions for members of the company's sales-force.

☐   **Social**: Events held with the aim of strengthening bonds between staff members or between representatives of the company and its key clients. For example, management retreats, team-building events and corporate hospitality days.

However they are classified, corporate events generally have three principal objectives: to educate; to inspire; and to provide the participants with opportunities for networking with each other. The proportions of these elements will vary according to the type of corporate event in question. For example, in incentive trips, inspiration and networking will be the dominant features; and in training sessions, the educational aspect will be prominent. But commentators generally agree that any organized gathering of colleagues and associates ought to feature each of these three characteristics in some measure.

Occasionally, company meetings are held on companies' own premises and are organised in-house, with little or no commercial significance for any stakeholders beyond the companies themselves. However, most companies recognise that in the main there are many compelling reasons for holding their meetings off-site. These include:

☐   a lack of capacity in their own premises (few company offices have facilities and the necessary audio-visual equipment for large meetings)

☐ the need to give staff a break from their normal working environment (to free them from day-to-day work-related distractions; to help them think more creatively, in a different setting)

☐ the wish to motivate staff by holding the meeting in an attractive location, possibly with leisure elements, such as golf or a spa

☐ the need to keep proceedings confidential, when, for example, sensitive topics, such as redundancies, are under discussion

☐ the need to meet on 'neutral' grounds, as, for instance, when representatives from two companies are meeting to discuss a merger.

■ Association meetings

Associations, federations, societies and clubs exist at different geographical levels, from local to global, and holding conferences annually – or at times more frequently – is one of the services that they offer their members, who attend in order to benefit from the education and networking activities on offer at such events. Attendance is voluntary, and generally paid for by the association member.

The association market covers a wide range of event types and categories: medical meetings (the largest segment); scientific; other academic; trade organisations; professional bodies; social groupings. In terms of size, budget, duration and complexity there are significant variations between and also within categories. Meetings of local associations such as Chambers of Commerce may attract only a dozen or so attendees, meeting in a local restaurant for a few hours. At the international level, such associations can attract a vast number of delegates to their events. For example, the annual conference of the European Society of Cardiology, the members of which are medical professionals specializing in cardiovascular diseases, regularly attracts over 20,000 delegates. This five-day event provides the delegates from all over Europe and beyond with an invaluable opportunity to meet together and exchange ideas and information on new challenges and new techniques related to the field of cardiovascular medicine.

However, according to the ICCA publication, *A Modern History of International Association Meetings*, most associations demonstrate the following common characteristics:

☐   Almost every 'specialty' has an association which holds one or more meetings.

☐   Most associations have meetings that are repeated at regular intervals. These can be annual, biennial etc.

☐   The destinations rotate. They rarely return to the same destination within very short time-span. The initiative to host a meeting often comes from the local counterpart, e.g. the national association. If that body is difficult to motivate to organise the meeting, the chances are high that the meeting will be scheduled elsewhere.

☐   Association meetings have a very long lead-time; it is not unusual to find lead-times of 5 years or more.

☐   It is estimated that a growing minority of about 25-30% of the decision-making processes no longer include an official bidding procedure, but have a 'central initiator' who selects the location and venues based on pre-determined and strict criteria. (More details on this aspect of association meetings are available from the ICCA publication, *International association meetings: bidding and decision-making for associations.*)

■   Government meetings

Meetings are held by governments and government departments at various geographical levels, from municipalities and regional government though to national/federal governments and transnational administrations such as the European Union. Many such meetings are for the purposes of debate and negotiation, but many are for the training of government employees.

At the high-profile end of the government meetings spectrum, such as summit conferences attended by heads of state and their entourages, security is a major factor to be taken into consideration in the choice of destination and venue. Memories of G8 conferences accompanied by rioting crowds of demonstrators are still fresh in the collective memory.

Although the security and hospitality costs of such events mean that budgets are lavish at times, these are the exceptions. For most routine government meetings, from policy launches to training events for civil servants, budgets are closely scrutinised, since it is public money that is being used. And the scrutiny and accountability of government meetings' travel has increased significantly in recent years.

A recent report by Rockport Analytics showed that in the US, government spending on meetings was less than half of the expenditure in the corporate sector.

The research showed that the US government spent about half as much on a per employee basis than the private sector – $737 per employee versus $1,531 for private industries.

Rockport also compared per diem delegate expenditures for travel and operations between the government and private sectors. In 2011, private sector per day meeting-initiated travel spending reached $224 per delegate, while government meetings attendees spent only $185 per day on travel, almost 20 percent less. Operations spending at government-hosted meetings was also found to be lower than in the private sector. Government spending on space rental, food & beverage, audio-visual, etc. was about $173 per meeting delegate, while the private sector spent $339 per delegate, nearly double that amount. According to Rockport Analytics, these differences can be explained by a number of factors:

☐   Government travel policy and mandated per diems dictate limits on average daily room rates, food &beverage spending, airfare and other categories. Private sector business travellers tend to have more latitude on travel purchases and travel policies with higher upper limits.

☐   Government meetings are often held at destinations, venues and with schedules that have lower cost profiles.

☐   Many privately sponsored meetings attended by government employees offer significant registration discounts and subsidised participating hotel room rates. In essence, government delegate attendance is important enough to meeting sponsors that a full or partial subsidy is offered.

■   SMERF events

The SMERF (Social Military, Educational, Religious and Fraternal) segment is a useful catch-all category, covering most types of meeting that are not held by professional/trade associations, companies or government organisations. In Holloway et al.'s *Business of Tourism*, the sub-segments are defined as follows:

☐ **Social meetings**: this segment includes all groups who meet primarily for social interaction, for instance, collectors, hobbyists, special interest groups, and family events such as weddings and bar mitzvahs.

☐ **Military meetings**: this segment largely comprises the reunions of people who served in the armed forces during periods of conflict. The intensity – and often the tragedy – that can characterise such events means that those who lived through them often find comfort in reuniting with their fellow fighters at regular intervals, to discuss their wartime experiences and commemorate their comrades who did not survive hostilities.

☐ **Educational meetings**: those who attend such events are generally teachers, lecturers and academic researchers who meet in order to share their research in their particular subject area, as well as new challenges and other developments affecting their teaching of their specialist subject.

☐ **Religious meetings**: some of the largest gatherings organised in the world's major cities are for the purpose of bringing together, for one or more days, people who share the same faith. At such events, worship and prayer are often combined with debates and workshops during which topical issues relating to the attendees' particular religion are discussed.

☐ **Fraternal meetings**: this segment includes primarily meetings of sororities, fraternities, and other fraternal organisations. University alumni reunions are a typical example of a fraternal meeting.

The distinguishing characteristics of SMERF events present opportunities as well as challenges for venues seeking to host them. In general, they are:

☐ Price-sensitive, regarding accommodation rates and venue rates, as attendees are generally self-funded; but they are more recession-proof than corporate meetings

☐ Organised by volunteers belonging to informal organisations or by family members – so the task of identifying them and marketing to them can be challenging

☐ Frequently held over weekends and in off-peak periods. This reduces the likelihood of a corporate meeting being disturbed by the noise coming from a wedding party in the same venue, but nevertheless the possibility of clashes of that kind is something that venue managers must take into account.

☐ Often held in second tier (non-capital) cities, for budgetary reasons

☐ Attended by people who are prepared to share rooms in order to reduce their personal expenses.

Writing in *Successful Meetings* magazine, Welly notes that: 'Conference centres are playing host to more and more SMERF events, particularly weddings, which can largely be attributed to two factors: the economic downturn, which has made conference centre sales staffs go after a more varied type of business; and the increasingly luxurious amenities available, which makes them more appealing destinations for weddings, family reunions, and those scrapbooking conventions'.

Benchmark Hospitality International is a privately held company that manages an extensive portfolio of resorts, conference centres and hotels. The company's senior vice president of sales and marketing, Ted Davis, is quoted by Welly as saying: 'Conference centres are very different than they were five years ago. They started as very serious meeting spaces. Now you have that serious approach if you want it, but they are set up more like luxury resorts.'

According to Davis, in one year alone, the SMERF market as a whole increased for Benchmark by 5 percent, with the religious market seeing the strongest gains at 12 percent, followed by the military market with gains of 8 percent. Gains of 15 percent in the wedding market, he said, were the result of both more sophisticated marketing and capital investments such as china, silver, and decor.

Many properties actively market themselves for weddings and social events by highlighting different features of the facility — which can extend to naming the venue differently for each market segment. Wellly gives an example of this, from one venue in Santa Cruz in California:

"We go by two different names, really. Fifteen years ago we used to be recognised as the Chaminade Executive Conference Center. We dropped "executive" for group business and we are really just known as Chaminade. For leisure business, including SMERF and weddings, we go by Chaminade Resort and Spa," says Sherrie Huneke, Chaminade's director of sales. The property does a brisk wedding business—averaging about 65 a year—but Huneke says that "the corporate market is our primary focus."

■ Marketing venues

It is the role of venue sales and marketing staff to maximize their occupancy and revenue by persuading meeting organisers to select their venue for events. This makes the sales and marketing department of any venue one of its most important departments. Venues that invest in effective sales techniques are likely to be rewarded for their efforts and increase their clientele, raise their profile and secure more bookings.

This process begins by gaining a thorough understanding of the market for meetings and what outcomes clients are seeking, from the events they hold. Venues are key suppliers in the meetings market, and – at the most basic level – they are in the business of enabling their clients achieve the best outcomes from their meetings and events.

This chapter has provided an overview of the main characteristics which differentiate the various market segments from each other, and it has been seen that the price that the different segments are willing to pay for venues is one of those characteristics.

Figure 1.3 displays the key characteristics of each market segment.

But it is not always the costs that affect the decisions around where to hold meetings and events. It can also very much depend on how a venue engages with its audiences from first time contact to post-event evaluation; how it markets itself through the quality of its communication tools; and how it approaches the task of face-to-face selling in different contexts. All of these techniques are vital in making that compelling first impression and gaining the confidence and trust of customers, in order to convince them that venue staff are professional, experienced and capable of working with them in partnership to ensure the success of their events.

The following chapters in this book point the way towards achieving that confidence and trust from all of the client segments discussed here.

Corporate

The process of deciding where to hold events is relatively straightforward.

The actual corporate meeting buyer may be difficult to identify within the initiator's organisation: secretaries, personal assistants, marketing executives, directors of training and many others may book corporate meetings.

Attendance is usually required of company employees

Lead times can be short.

Events typically last from 1 – 2 days.

A higher budget per delegate.

Venues used: hotels, management training centres, unusual venues.

Delegates'partners are rarely invited, except in the case of incentive trips

Association

The process of choosing a destination can be prolonged.

A committee is usually involved in the choosing of the destination; and the organizers may be volunteers from the association's membership.

Attendance is voluntary.

The annual convention may be booked many years in advance.

Events typically last from 2 – 4 days.

A lower budget per delegate, since for some attendees, price is a sensitive issue and they may be paying their own costs

Venues used: conference centres, civic and academic venues.

Delegates' partners frequently attend

Government

Considerable variety in terms of length of event and budgets available.

However, budgets are usually scrutinised, since public money is being used.

High security measures are indispensable: these meetings are frequently accompanied by demonstrations and disruption.

Smerf

Price-sensitive, regarding accommodation rates and venue rates; but more recession-proof than corporate meetings

Held by organisations that are run by volunteers – so the task of identifying them can be challenging

Frequently held over weekends and in off-peak periods

Often held in 2nd-tier cities, using simple accommodation and facilities

Attended by delegates who bring their spouses/families and are likely to extend their trips, for leisure purposes

Figure 1.3: Market segments and their distinguishing features, Source: Davidson and Rogers (2006)

Contrasting market segments at the Florida Aquarium

The Florida Aquarium (www.flaquarium.org) located in Tampa, Florida, is a large scale, 23,000 m2 aquarium that is home to over 20,000 aquatic plants and animals from all over the world. The aquarium is a not-for-profit organisation and is operated by the public sector.

While the Florida Aquarium is best known as a world-class tourist attraction, it is also an established education resource (it received its 1,000,000th student visitor in 2011) and a research and conservation facility with current projects on coral propagation, underwater archaeology and sea turtle rescue and rehabilitation.

In addition, the aquarium's facilities are available for hire for a range of events. Jason Carroll, Director of Sales & Events, describes the advantages and challenges of focusing on a non-business segments of the events market.

One of the greatest lessons I have learned in my time working for The Florida Aquarium is that when the economy fails….weddings are recession-proof! Our Aquarium used to only do about 10 weddings a year when I started here. The majority of our business was convention groups, and local corporate events. When the crisis hit the national and international economy and the US housing market collapsed, we lost about 70% of that business. So, instead of reducing our prices and begging for the little corporate and convention business that was left, as our competitors did, we refocused our business to concentrate on the wedding market and we now do over 100 weddings a year. We have increased our revenues every year and never really suffered when others did, during the economic crisis. I didn't realise this before, but I now understand that the wedding business is resistant to recession.

We changed the focus of all of our advertising, stopping all print ads and spending all of the allocated advertising budget on wedding websites such as theknot.com, weddingwire.com, and gatheringguide.com We also packaged our venue with food & beverage options that made it much easier for the prospective couple to purchase a wedding with the Aquarium. We found that prior to the package only 30% of our booked weddings were ordering an open bar at their weddings. When we instituted the packages that number jumped to 90% of weddings hosting the bar at their wedding. This increased the per capita for food & beverage at our events by 27%

in the first year. In addition, liquor has a high profit margin so we noticed a sizeable increase in the bottom line as well. We also reorganised the staffing of our events department. We originally had sales people and event coordinators. The sales people would book the business and then turn it over to an events coordinator. Instead, we now have Sales & Event Coordinators who both sell clients the wedding package, then work with them the whole time to plan and execute it. This has been very successful for us and we get enthusiastic reviews about the process.

However, there is a down side. We find that a wedding event will take approximately 50% more time to coordinate and plan than a non-wedding event. We have had to reapportion our staff to accommodate for this, changing the sales and operation structure of the department.

To plan a corporate event usually entails one site tour, 2-3 phone calls, then 5-10 e-mails. A wedding event takes a site tour, 3 onsite planning meetings of one hour each, 10-15 phone calls, and 40-50 e-mails to plan. We also find that these clients do not have much experience of planning events, so we spend time teaching them about what will work and what will not and must provide explanations for these suggestions. Our corporate clients, on the other hand, are much more experienced at planning events and we don't find ourselves teaching them along the way in the same way we have to do with our social clients. In addition, the planning of wedding involves a strong emotional aspect with wedding clients. This means that we need to listen to them describe all of the intricate relationships within their families; and why, for example, some people can't be seated next to certain other people; and the whole history of why they are making particular planning decisions, etc. And all of this takes precious time.

Sources

Beech J, Kaiser S and Kaspar R (2013) *The Business of Events Management*, Pearson Education, Harlow

CIC (2011) *The Economic Significance of Meetings to the US Economy*, Convention Industry Council

Davidson R and Rogers T (2006) *Marketing Destinations and Venues for Conferences, Conventions and Business Events*, Butterworth Heinemann

Eades, R and Brewerton, A (eds) (2008) *The Future of Booking Venues*, HBAA

Holloway J C, Humphreys C and Davidson R (2009) *The Business of Tourism*, Pearson Education

IAPCO (2013) Online Dictionary, International Association of Professional Congress Organizers

ICCA (2012) *A Modern History of International Association Meetings*, International Congress and Convention Association

ICCA (2013) *International association meetings: bidding and decision-making for associations*, International Congress and Convention Association

Jago L and Deery M (2010) *Delivering Innovation, Knowledge and Performance: The Role of Business Events*, Business Events Council of Australia

JMIC (2009) Key Messages for the Meetings Industry, Joint Meetings Industry Council

Minton E (2005) 'What planners really want', in *The Meeting Professional*, June

Rockport Analytics (2013) *The Value of Government Meetings*

Rogers T (2013) *Conferences and Conventions*, 3rd Edition, Routledge

Segar A (2009) *Conferences That Work: Creating Events That People Love*, www.conferencesthatwork.com

UNWTO (2006) *Measuring the Economic Importance of the Meetings Industry – Developing a Tourism Satellite Account Extension*, United Nations World Tourism Organization

Welly K (2011) Conference Centers Get SMERF-Happy, *Successful Meetings*, March 1

Online sources of further information

Business Events Sydney: Beyond Tourism Benefits: Measuring the social legacy of business events
www.businesseventssydney.com.au/about-us/publications-and-resources/research-studies/

Smartmeetings.com: SMERF: the Market Stabilizer
http://smartmeetings.com/event-planning-magazine/2013/03/smerf-the-market-stabilizer

Why Face-to-Face Business Meetings Matter: A White Paper by Professor Richard D. Arvey, Ph.D. Business School, National University of Singapore
www.iacconline.org/content/files/WhyFace-to-FaceBusinessMeetingsMatter.pdf

International Congress and Convention Association (ICCA): A Modern History of International Association meetings
www.iccaworld.com/dcps/doc.cfm?docid=1626

2 Sources of Business

The leads database

A lead is a person, business, or organization that is potentially interested in the products or services that a business offers.

New sales leads are the lifeblood of most businesses. Collecting business leads, qualifying them and then following them up with the aim of converting them into paying customers is an ongoing and essential task for any company aiming to find new customers. It is a task that requires skill, money, and that most precious of business assets, time. Figure 2.1 shows the process in the form of a diagram, as the Purchase Funnel (also called the Sales Funnel, or Decision Funnel) which is a framework that illustrates the diminishing number of potential customers that get through each subsequent stage of the process.

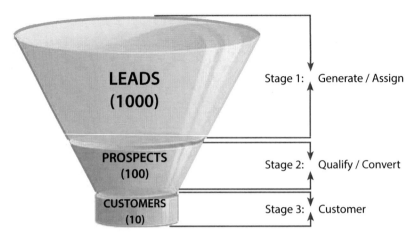

Figure 2.1: The Purchase Funnel

The process begins by generating business leads (Stage 1) – actively collecting details of potential customers and recording them, organizing them and storing them in an electronic database in such a way that they can be used in order to manage the leads as part of the sales and marketing process. The essential elements to be recorded include each lead's:

☐ Name

☐ Title

☐ Name of their company or organisation

☐ Telephone number

☐ Email address

☐ What it is that qualifies the individual or company as a lead.

However, these are only the most basic details required for each lead, and more comprehensive information on each lead should be recorded, if known. This might include the number and type of events that they organise and the frequency of those events, as well as the market segment they represent (corporate, association, government, and so on). In fact any additional information available about the lead that is relevant and that could prove to be useful in converting them into paying customers should be recorded. This might extend to personal information such as the fact that the lead enjoys playing golf or even their birthday or their children's names. All such information can be useful in building a relationship with the lead.

An extensive and up-to-date database composed of the details of large numbers of business leads is a significant asset for most venues and an invaluable resource for its salespeople. It is also a resource that needs to be not only created but managed: 'cleaned' from time to time, to eliminate obsolete leads or to update their details. This form of database management can be a time-consuming activity, and for that reason, venues sometimes employ a researcher or an intern to work on this aspect of sales. But whether managed by a member of the venue staff or by someone recruited specifically for that purpose, it is clear that a key step in the venue sales process is that of creating and managing a leads database in an effective, operational manner.

This chapter begins by examining the many ways in which leads can be generated and collected by sales staff, to be added to the venue's database. There follows a consideration of the process of qualifying these leads (Stage 2 in Figure 2.1). Chapter 3 begins by analyzing how the Account Management process can be used in order to turn qualified leads into customers of the venue (Stage 3 in Figure 2.1).

■ Clients already known to the venue

Before exploring the various sources of new leads for venues, it is worth considering those people who have already been in contact with the venue, and whose potential to generate business is often overlooked.

A crucial discussion between any venue and their client is that which is held during the follow-up meeting that takes place just after the client's event, for the purpose of reviewing how the event was handled by the venue. In order to be most effective, these meetings should encourage a 2-way exchange of views, with the venue giving feedback to their client, as well as soliciting their opinions on the venue's performance. This means that the venue manager needs firstly to consult other staff within the venue (for example, Food & Beverage, Security and Reception) to get their perspectives on how the event was run. If there were any problems, they will be already known to the venue manager if he or she has been in contact with the client throughout the day of their event. (Even if it is not their role to actually run the event, its good practice for the venue manager to at least see their client at some point or points throughout the day to check on how their event is going). If any problems have arisen, the end-of-day follow-up meeting provides an opportunity for both sides to propose solutions.

But the value of these meetings goes beyond their significance as sources of useful feedback for both venue and client. This is also the best moment for the venue to ask satisfied clients:

☐ to provide them with testimonials, written or filmed, which can – with the client's permission – be posted on the venue's website and used in other marketing materials.

☐ what other business the client may have to place in the future, and to agree when the venue may get in touch with the client to discuss that.

☐ for referrals. Will they provide the contact details of anyone else they know who plans events, either in other departments or branches in their own organisation or in other organisations altogether? This is the beginning of the account management process.

■ Former clients

While it is gratifying to win business from clients who have not already booked an event with the venue, a potential source of business that is often overlooked are former clients – clients who stopped making bookings after one experience of using the venue and those once-regular customers who ceased holding their events there.

Effective account management includes firstly investigating the reasons that explain why such clients discontinued their use of the venue and secondly attempting to rekindle their interest. There may be many reasons for them not coming back:

☐ the client had a disappointing experience of using the venue

☐ there was a change of personnel and the person who used to happily book the venue has been replaced by someone who is unaware of it

☐ the client's company or organisation relocated in another part of the country

☐   their workforce or membership has grown to the extent that they have had to seek a larger venue

☐   their meeting was a one-off event only

☐   there was a change of venue sales staff, and the new manager is unaware of this client

2

☐   the client did not think that their event worked well at the venue (but this should prompt the venue to offer alternative solutions)

But it could also as simple as the venue failing to follow up and ask the client for more business. It could be that they simply need reminding that the venue is still in business and interested in their custom.

Whatever the reason, it is worth contacting the client to find out, and to see if they may be persuaded to use the venue again. Former clients offer the advantage of already knowing the venue, therefore less time is needed to explain to them its features and procedures.

If a significant amount of time has passed since they last placed business with the venue, the client should be updated on any developments in the venue (a refurbishment, a new product, or a special offer, for example). These can provide an additional reason for the client to come back.

A key part of account management would consist of requesting a meeting with past clients to discuss any new developments and also how their requirements may have changed. One of the objectives of such a meeting would be for the venue manager to suggest alternative, additional ways in which the venue might be used by the client. For example they may have held their Annual General Meeting in the venue, but are unaware that it can also accommodate dinners.

Unrealised business

Most venues hold data on potential clients whose business was unrealized. There are two types of unrealized business:

☐   Enquiries regarding a specific event which were turned down by the venue (known as 'refused business'). This may have been because the venue had no availability on the desired dates; or the enquirer's requirements did not quite fit the venue; or the enquirer's budget was too low. In any case, the reason for the refusal should be recorded in the venue's database, as this is information that could be useful in future negotiations with the prospect. If the problem was one of availability of the prospect's desired dates, they should be contacted in the event of any subsequent cancellation that releases the venue for those dates, to see if the prospect is still looking for a venue.

☐   Potential clients who held space provisionally at the venue, either on a first or second option, but then released it, usually because either their event did not go ahead or they decided to hold the event in another venue instead (known as 'released business'). It is always good policy for the venue to find out why the space was released. For example, if it transpires that it is because the prospect was offered a better price in another venue, this could be a prompt towards further negotiation with the prospect, on the basis of price.

Venues can contact these people to find out the reasons behind their choice – if the question was not put to them at the actual time when they refused or released. Such prospects represent a valuable source of potential business, because they made an initial enquiry to the venue, indicating an interest in it. Therefore it makes good sense to contact them to determine what other events they may have in the pipeline and whether they may be persuaded to make a future booking. As with all prospects, they can be asked when they are likely to be planning events in the future, so that, at the very least, the venue manager can make a note to contact them again around that date.

It is clear that those contacts already on the venue's database can be a fruitful source of business. But all businesses need to constantly add new leads to their database in order to open up new markets. All of the following methods can be effective in generating new leads for venues.

Sources of new leads

■ Commercial databases

Buying a ready-made list is the fastest way of adding large numbers
of leads to a venue's database. Bought-in data of this type may be purchased from a number of sources:

□ **Commercial companies.** 'Lead brokers' and 'lead companies'
generate leads and then sell them to companies looking for
sources of new business. For any venue choosing to supplement
their database in this way, it is essential to work with a reputable
company to avoid wasting time following up inappropriate or
obsolete leads.

□ **Meetings industry publications.** Many meetings industry
publications create databases of their subscribers who have opted
to receive third-party communications. For example, in the UK,
Meetings & Incentive Travel (M&IT) magazine maintains a database
of over 16,000 email addresses of conference and events buyers
in the UK and overseas. The database is structured in such a way
that it allows users to contact the leads according to geographical
location and/or type of buyer.

□ **Meetings industry associations.** One of the benefits of membership of some associations of meetings industry professionals is
access to their marketing databases. For example, the Association
Database of ICCA, the International Congress and Convention
Association, lists the details of the regular conferences of over
13,000 international associations. It gives a historical overview
of each meeting listed, creating a complete track record of where
it has been held in the past and the destinations that have been
chosen for the future. The information also includes several
contact addresses of local key contacts as well as meeting venues
requirements, decision procedures and destinations which may be
eligible for the future. Membership of MPI, Meeting Professionals
International provides access to 22,000 meetings industry professionals across the globe.

□ **Chambers of Commerce and professional associations.** Lists
of local businesses can often be bought from Chambers of

Commerce. Some may be organised according to a system that, for example, allows the identification of people with 'event manager' in their title within specific geographical parameters. Some professional associations charge for access to the database of their membership. By using this method, prospects such as training managers and human resources managers can be contacted en masse.

Most venue managers agree that the use of purchased databases can be a cost-effective way of finding significant numbers of new leads. But working with such leads demands considerable investment in terms of staff time, as the contacts on these lists are usually completely 'cold', having no prior relationship with the purchaser of the list.

There are many methods that venues can employ to build up a leads database, and the rest of this chapter examines the ways of doing this by using sources of new leads

■   Desk research

The press – hard-copy and online

For venues that are targeting the local market for meetings and events, the local or regional press can be a useful source of information on new business openings and expansions as well as new personnel and promotions of key people. A new business opening up in the vicinity of the venue may need meeting rooms for the interviewing and training of new staff, for example.

Internet searches

The Internet provides venues with an invaluable tool for conducting searches on particular market segments or individual companies, to expand their own databases. For example, venue staff can search online for information on:

☐   different market segments such pharmaceuticals, information technology firms, or financial services and their related associations

☐   specific company details and contact information, the types of venues they use for their events

☐   managers, across a range of companies, with responsibility for choosing venues. For example, for a training venue wishing to target HR professionals in the local area, the internet can be an extremely effective research tool.

The Social Media

With the advent of social networking sites such as Facebook, Twitter and LinkedIn, the world of business networking is as much about online interacting as the more traditional, face to face offline gatherings.

For example, use of the Advanced Search function of Linkedin is one of the most powerful free tools available for lead generation – for finding new leads or simply locating previous customers that may have moved to new companies. By adding the appropriate search criteria – key words, such as for example, 'events' + 'planner', as well as the relevant geographical range, a list of Linkedin subscribers matching those criteria is instantly produced. These leads can be added to the venue's database to be followed up, either through Linkedin or through other means of communication.

Going further, the LinkedIn Premium service offers the ability to search by the following characteristics:

☐   function

☐   seniority

☐   interests

☐   years of experience

☐   company size

The use of the social media for marketing purposes by venue is further explored in Chapter 7.

Venue websites

Within the past decade, there has been a major and rapid move to online tools, in terms of the methods that meeting planners use when seeking and evaluating potential venues for their events. Online is where new prospects tend to go first, if they are conducting a general search for a venue. As a response to this trend, many venues no longer use printed brochures, but, instead, seek to maximize the effectiveness of their online presence, notably through their websites and the use of e-brochures. The website has become the main shop-front for most venues. Effectively-designed websites can generate enquires and build venues' leads databases whenever the following techniques are used to drive visitors to the websites:

☐ **Directing responses to promotional efforts** such as e-mail marketing campaigns and advertising campaigns to the venue's website (as well as to a telephone number at the venue)

☐ **Blogging**. A weekly blog by one or more members of the venue's staff can drive additional traffic to the website, if it adds value to visitors by providing them with useful, interesting or simply amusing content. This does not mean a description of the venue's facilities and services. Instead, the blog should cover topics that visitors enjoy reading and can use in their work. For example, Sydney Convention and Exhibition Centre's blog topics (http://blog.scec.com.au/) range from practical items such as 'Five ways to use LinkedIn to skyrocket your event attendance' and 'Attention! How to excite and charm today's easily bored event delegates' to humorous posts such as 'Nine strange items brought into, or left behind at, the Centre'. Meeting planners welcome tips and advice on a whole range of topics from green meetings and hybrid meetings to how to organize an event on a budget and even how to choose wines for a gala dinner.

☐ **Publishing research reports**. Going one step further, some venues find it useful to commission and publish research reports on subjects of interest to meeting planners and make them available for download on their websites.

Most venues also find it useful to have a presence on third-party websites that link straight through to the venue's own website. This is because meeting planners often go directly to these third-party websites to conduct their venue searches and input their search criteria. Venues that satisfy those criteria then show up in the search. For example, the Cvent Supplier Network offers a public database of more than 200,000 venues worldwide.

Whatever the motivation for people visiting the venue's website, they should be encouraged to leave their email addresses and other information about themselves, if possible, so that these can be added to the venue's database and followed up by sales staff. But it is important to ensure the visitors know how the information will be used and they should usually be given the option of not submitting their details (except, of course, when they are submitting an enquiry).

Given that, for any venue, their website is now a key factor in attracting the attention of clients and prospects and persuading them to make a booking, it is vital to consider what, in terms of design and content, makes an effective website.

There are a number of features that should be present and apparent to any visitor:

☐ **The website should be kept simple and clear** so that visitors can navigate through it quickly and find the information that they are looking for. Too much text can slow down the visitor in their search.

☐ One of the first details that visitors to the site should see is the **location of the venue**. To indicate the venue's location, a map graphic can be included on the homepage and even in the sidebar of all interior pages.

☐ It should be possible for visitors to the website to **download everything they need** – floor plans, exhibitor manuals, health and safety regulations, and so on.

☐ **Testimonials** (with permission) from previous, satisfied, clients are always persuasive, because meeting planners tend to believe what other meeting planners say about venues – more than they believe what venue sales staff say! Short testimonials, featuring past clients saying how pleased they were with their experience of holding their event in the venue, how satisfied their delegates were, etc, can either be in writing (a paragraph is generally long enough), accompanied if possible by a head-and-shoulders photograph of the meeting planner; or it could even be a video testimonial: a one-minute movie of the meeting planner expressing their satisfaction with the venue. Production standards matter less than what is actually said. Some venues simply sit their client in front of a laptop camera and ask them to speak about how their event went.

☐ **Case-studies of successful events** hosted in the venue. Detailed descriptions of recent events that the venue has hosted can be an effective way of demonstrating the range of clients who use the venue and the ability of the venue to be flexible in accommodating a variety of events in terms of size, client segment and purpose. Case-studies can be enhanced by including images of the events hosted as well as testimonials (again, with permission) from organisers and even from participants.

☐ **Virtual tours of the venue**. Well-produced, 360-degree videos of the venue, inside and out are not only eye-catching, but also effective in allowing potential clients to explore meeting rooms and public areas on their own computers and other devices. The impact is heightened when the viewer of the video can use the controls on their keyboard to control their tour of the venue. Short movies of events held in the venue can also be eye-catching and illustrative of how the venue can be used.

☐ **An online enquiry form**. A simple form that visitors to the website can complete in order to get answers to any questions they may have about the venue is a useful way of moving potential clients on to the next stage of their enquiry. The form should be easy to complete, without too many questions. Drop-down boxes work well, with a section for any additional comments. (It goes without saying that such enquiries should be followed up as soon as possible).

☐ Venues offering 'simple' products such as boardrooms that can be fairly standardised across, for example, properties belonging to the same hotel chain, may offer the **option of online booking** of such facilities. However, for most venues the complexity of the facilities they offer rules out the possibility of including the option of online booking on their websites, as some form of human intervention is generally required to facilitate the booking process.

■ ## Other enquirers

Almost anyone who contacts a venue by other means, such as by telephone, email, or (more rarely) visiting in person or sending a letter, seeking general information are a potential source of business, and should therefore have their details added to the leads database. These are people who have read about or heard about the venue and chose to get in touch for further details. It is sound policy to ask, in the first place, where they heard about the venue, as this will give some indication as to where the venue's marketing budget is being spent most effectively. It may not be appropriate to start selling to such enquirers at the time of the initial enquiry – it is important to gauge the conversation and let the enquirer go if they appear to be getting impatient. But it is absolutely acceptable to contact them again at a later date, and adding them to the database allows for this option.

■ Referrals from other venues

Another important source of leads can come in the form of referrals from venues' own competitors. Occasionally, groups of venues in the same locality create an informal referral system between themselves, so that if, for whatever reason, one venue in the group cannot accommodate an event, they refer it on to the others. Although it may at first glance appear counter-intuitive to help one's competitors in this way, the client will usually appreciate being referred; and if the act of referral is reciprocated in the future, the system generates goodwill between all parties and becomes win-win-win. This provides a sound reason for venue managers not only to get to know their competing venues but also to stay on friendly terms with them.

■ Marketing consortia and venue associations

Going a step beyond the setting up of informal referral systems, many venues join together to create their own marketing consortia which offer meeting planners the possibility of contacting any member of the consortium through a central enquiry point – usually a website or Members' Directory. Such venues usually share some similarity with each other, which provides the rationale for creating the consortium in the first place. For example, The Westminster Collection (www.venues-london.co.uk) has established itself as an influential marketing consortium for 47 iconic venues within Westminster in central London, including Westminster Abbey, the London Transport Museum and Imperial College. The organisation's marketing support services are designed to bolster their member venues' own marketing activities and generate new business leads. To facilitate this, their website offers an online venue enquiry service, for events organisers and agencies.

Venues interested in collaborating with similar venues in this way but unable to find a suitable consortium always have the option of creating a new one – even if it begins with just three venues.

An interesting example of this was the creation of the London City Selection (LCS), at www.londoncityselection.co.uk. LCS was set up initially by a small number of venues seeking to work more collaboratively with each other. All of them are unique venues within the City of London that in some way complement each other. To facilitate their cooperation with each other, these venues set up a referral system and developed a website. The website is now the main driver of business into the LCS, and the referral system ensures that business stays within the member venues. It has been highly successful and now has 26 venues within its membership.

Venue associations

Venue associations bringing together venues that share a particular characteristic represent another source of leads for their members. For example, Historic Conference Centres of Europe (www.hcce.com) is a marketing-focused association that promotes 26 conference and convention centres in heritage buildings in 13 European countries. Such associations generally have a broader role than simply marketing their members to potential customers and acting as an enquiry point: for example, the education and training of their members, benchmarking, staff exchange programmes or lobbying governments and other decision-makers on their behalf. But it is their potential to be valuable sources of new business that encourages many venues to become members.

The International Association of Conference Centres (www.iacconline.org) is another example of a venue association that offers its members a range of useful sales and marketing support services. The 300+ venues worldwide that meet IAAC's exacting standards for membership enjoy a wide range of benefits that include a full-page listing on the association's website, with a Request for Proposal (RFP) link to facilitate enquiries from meeting planners; and a listing in the IACC Global Membership Directory, which is distributed to over 14,000 qualified meeting planners annually, on a global basis.

■ Attending events

Even in the age of electronic communication, the quality of the relationships between buyers and suppliers remains of paramount importance. As the saying goes, 'people buy people', and opportunities for face-to-face networking offered by attendance at live events enable venue staff (all venue staff, not only sales and marketing) to meet people who are potential sources of business.

2

Meetings industry events

In most countries with a developed meetings industry, there are regular events that create the opportunity for venues to meet potential clients on an informal basis. These would include the annual conferences of the national or international meetings industry associations, as well as the more frequent educational events run by those associations, such as the evening events run by the various chapters of Meeting Professionals International. At such events, the participants not only learn something of relevance to their profession but also engage in networking activities. The various national and regional awards ceremonies for the meetings industry also provide an environment where initial contacts can be made between venues and prospects or where existing relationships between them can be reinforced.

Going one step further, venues may decide to sponsor an element of these events as a public relations exercise to reinforce their brand. By sponsoring, for example, a drinks reception or a lunch, venues can gain special recognition that raises their profile with an audience that includes potential clients. The Barbican in London once sponsored the annual conference of the Association of British Professional Conference Organisers by hosting it, free of charge, in their venue. This meant that for the duration of the event, over 200 meeting planners were able to experience the venue's facilities and services and see at first hand how they could be used to bring their events to life.

Client events

The opportunity to network with potential clients certainly makes meetings industry events worth attending, for venue staff. But it is widely acknowledged that only a small minority of the prospects that venues need to meet actually attend such events and that a strong case can be made for venue sales staff attending the type of events that directly attract their prospects in far greater numbers. For example, a venue wishing to target human resources managers as a potential source of training event bookings would almost certainly get significant return on investment from attending or exhibiting at a conference of Human Resources professionals. Venue managers therefore may find it beneficial to think outside the meetings industry by participating in events designed primarily for their target groups such as human resources professionals, association administrators and training managers, all of whom have their own associations that hold regular conferences and other events.

Events run at the venue

Venues can create events in their own properties to attract potential clients. These are events that go beyond simple site inspections (see Chapter 5) for meeting planners, although a tour of the venue can always be offered as an add-on. The event must offer something of direct interest to the participants, as attendance takes some of their time, their most valuable resource. Some venues create an advisory board that meets regularly in the venue to discuss meeting planners' experiences and expectations. As well as being a valuable source of information that venues can use in their business marketing plans, advertising collateral development, and managing the on-site meeting experience, the meetings of advisory boards familiarise the members with the venue and the venue staff. Some venues organise regular lunches or dinners to which potential clients are invited. These not only provide venue staff with quality time with their prospects, but also allow the venue to showcase their food and beverage offer in a direct way. Venues have also been known to hold an annual dinner or reception where they invite all clients and potential clients as an effective way of thanking them and also showcasing any new initiatives.

Whatever the event, there must be a clear business reason given for the guests to attend, if they are to get permission from their managers to take time off work to visit the venue. Given the pressure on people's time, evening events can be more popular than those held during office hours. It is important to achieve a good balance between numbers of members of staff and guests. Some form of follow-up after the event is also vital. By attending the event the prospects have experienced an initial connection with the venue, therefore when sales staff get back in touch with them after the event, this is no longer a case of cold-calling.

Kellogg Conference Center monthly client luncheon

2

The Kellogg Conference Centre, Washington DC. Photo © Kellogg Conference Centre

David Kohlasch, General Manager of the Kellogg Conference Center describes his venue's technique for developing relationships with prospects:

The venue and the challenge

The Kellogg Conference Center (http://kelloggconferencehotel.com) is located at Gallaudet University in Washington D.C. and is run by Flik International. The property needed more of a presence and visibility in the D.C. market place. Our goal was to get as many potential clients into our property to see how great it is.

The solution

We decided to host a monthly client luncheon and invite potential clients to join us for a great lunch and presentation about our property. We make it fun and relaxing; no high pressure sales. The luncheons are also an opportunity for the potential clients to meet our staff. We make sure that we showcase our entire staff, not just the sales team. We introduce one member of each department at our presentation; the staff appreciates it and our clients see that it is a team effort to service their events

Results

The results have been outstanding. We have increased our revenues dramatically and have developed excellent relationships with new clients. This was very easy to measure, as we reviewed the bookings from the clients that attend our luncheons and saw what additional revenues had been added.

Lessons

- Great food will attract people to a venue for site visits.

- The presentation needs to be unique and exciting.

- It is important to be creative and demonstrate talent.

- It is vital to showcase the entire team and introduce line staff to the audience.

- Follow-up after the luncheon with all clients is essential.

■ Workshops and forums

A more structured type of event for bringing together venues and prospects are the many workshops and forums that are created for this specific purpose and run on a regular basis, usually annually. Such events are organised on the basis of pre-qualification on both sides: buyers are qualified by the organisers, and suppliers can request appointments with certain buyers. Most workshops and forums offer one-on-one table-top appointments of a fixed duration (often 15 minutes) during which venues get the opportunity to ask precise qualifying questions about the prospects' needs. These events can be cost-effective in terms of funds and time invested, and, if well organised, can introduce participating venues to substantial numbers of prospects.

For example, Haymarket Events, a division of the global media company, Haymarket, runs five forums a year under the C&IT (Conference & Incentive Travel) brand, allowing key industry suppliers to meet UK agencies, European agencies, the top corporate event planners and the UK and international association markets. These are either one and a half day or two and a half day events, bringing together no more than 50 client delegates with 25 supplier companies for a series of pre-arranged meetings, lunches, dinners and a full workshop programme.

Occasionally, such events last longer, when they are combined with a fam (familiarisation) trip. An example of this was the C&IT Middle East Forum that ran from 28 September – 3 October 2013 and was hosted by the Abu Dhabi Convention Bureau and Etihad Airways. Forty UK senior-level events organisers with an interest in the Middle East as a destination travelled, free of charge, to Abu Dhabi for one and a half days of networking and one-to-one meetings and workshops with suppliers, many of whom were hotel venues such as the Starwood brands, Intercontinental Group IHG and Hilton Hotels, who have properties in that region. Other suppliers were unusual venues such as Ferrari World Abu Dhabi and the Yas Waterworld. Following the forum, participants enjoyed a fam trip of the region.

■ Friends and families

National cultures differ in the extent to which business life and private life interrelate and overlap. But in those countries where there is little aversion to allowing work-related matters to encroach into personal life, members of venue staff's families and circles of friends can become valuable sources of leads that may result in actual bookings. Friends and adult members of the extended families of venue employees may regularly attend meetings run by, for example, their employers or the professional associations to which they belong. By harnessing the power of word-of-mouth and encouraging venue staff to promote their place of employment as a venue for such events, this under-used source of business can be effectively exploited. Naturally, the 'hard-sell' approach is inappropriate in most situations outside employees' working life, but venue staff can be encouraged to introduce into their social conversations a casual mention of what they do and where they work, using a memorable elevator pitch. If those friends and family members are clear about what venue staff do and how they can help, they are better able to make qualified referrals.

■ Exhibitions

One of the most effective methods of adding new leads to any venue's database is by attending meetings industry exhibitions. Chapter 6 examines these business events in detail.

The leads qualification process

It is clear that a venue's database of leads is not an end in itself, but only the first stage in the sales process. The overall aim is not simply to find leads but, of course, to make sales. Generating leads is only the first step. The second step, the one that makes the leads database profitable and worth the effort, is to communicate with the leads in order to promote them from the status of leads to that of clients – those who finally purchase the company's product or service. Therefore, the process of lead generation should be followed by the process of lead qualification – ranking leads according to how likely they are to make a purchase.

The qualifying process may take place in various settings in which the venue's representative is communicating directly with the lead. This may be during a face-to-face meeting at an exhibition, or during a telephone sales call, for example. From the venue's perspective, the aim is to ask a number of qualifying questions that will determine the extent to which the lead is likely to use the venue's facilities and services for their events – and therefore the extent to which the sales team should invest time and energy in nurturing a relationship with the lead. The answers to all of these qualifying questions should, of course, be recorded in the leads database.

But the qualifying process is also an opportunity for the venue's representative to engage with the lead and begin the process of convincing him or her that the venue can satisfy their needs for meeting space and services. In order to ignite the lead's interest in this way, the venue representative needs to have a finely tuned 'elevator pitch' available. An elevator pitch is a brief, persuasive speech that can be used to spark interest in what any business does. A good elevator pitch should last no longer than a short elevator ride of 20 to 30 seconds, hence the name. Elevator pitches should be interesting, memorable, and succinct. In the context of qualifying a venue's leads, they also need to explain what makes the venue unique and why there is a close match between its services and facilities and those required by the lead.

In order to draw attention to the similarities between the lead's requirements and what the venue has to offer, it is essential that the venue representative conducts prior research into the lead and their organization, before the first contact. Research will help identify the clearest synergies between the venue and the lead, which will give the lead more of a reason to want to further the conversation with the venue and explore ways in which they can work together. For example, if the research reveals that the company runs an annual series of graduate training seminars, and the venue has a number of training rooms, then this is an obvious synergy to be mentioned by the lead's representative. Similarly, if the venue is a building of considerable architectural interest, then that clear connection with the architectural and design industries is something than can be emphasized when dealing with leads in those industry sectors. Or if the venue is located in a city with universities with a high reputation for medical research, it can also capitalise on those strengths in qualifying discussions with leads. It is important to highlight such synergies, as this will give the contact more of a reason to want to further the conversation with the venue and explore ways in which they can work together.

Finally, it should be noted that any venue representative at the stage of qualifying leads should have already established that the person they are speaking to is, if fact, the real decision maker within his or her organisation. This may be information that is already known to them, from the initial leads generation stage, or it can be obtained through research conducted either on the telephone, via email or on the internet.

Some of the most useful qualifying questions are shown in Figure 2.2.

1. The lead's events

What type of events does the lead hold?

What are the lead's general objectives for holding their events? How do they judge the success of their events?

How frequently are their events held? (Is there scope for repeat business?)

Who are their delegates? (What is the 'personality' of their group? Young, fun-seeking? Conservative?)

What is the average size of the events, how many delegates?

How many days?

What format and set up do they usually have?

What catering do they usually provide for delegates?

What are their usual audio-visual requirements?

How confidential are their meetings?

How much free time do delegates generally have?

2. The dates

At what times of the year / days of the week are their events held?

How flexible can the lead be with their days and dates?

If the venue was able to offer a better deal on an alternative date, would that be of interest?

Do they already have any dates for discussion?

3. Destinations and venues

What is important to the lead about the venues and destinations they select?

What other venues/destinations have they used previously?

What was their experience like?

What types of venues do they usually use?

What other venues are they considering?

Do they require accommodation?

Where will their delegates be traveling from?

4. The decision

When is the decision taken, on the choice of destination/venue?

Who makes the final decision? Who else has an influence on that decision?

Who is the main events organiser?

When would be a good time to come for a site inspection?

5. The budget

What kind of budget is made available for the lead's events?

How important is price, in the lead's choice of venue?

Is there a possibility of the lead holding several meetings at the venue as part of a multi-year deal, in return for a discounted rate?

Figure 2.2: Qualifying Questions

Venue sales and venue marketing

This book focuses primarily on venue sales techniques, but it is worth mentioning here that sales and marketing go hand-in-hand for any venue. Ultimately all of a venue's marketing activities are tasked with the aim of raising awareness and driving sales for the venue. All sales activity should therefore be supported by the venue's marketing and communications efforts, whether those consist of direct mail, website marketing, press advertising, sponsorship and branding opportunities, award entries, corporate gifts or any other techniques for raising clients' awareness of the venue.

Public Relations is another important element of marketing that is closely linked with the sales function of a venue. PR is not just about profile and branding, it can also have a significant and direct impact on sales, and in that respect is directly linked to business growth.

All such marketing should be strictly in line with the objectives and values of the venue and closely related to the target markets which the venue has identified.

The distinction is often made between strategic marketing and strategic sales. Strategic marketing provides the prospects and leads while strategic sales close the deals to provide the revenue that keeps businesses operating.

In the case of small venues or non-traditional venues, the same person may be fulfilling both roles. However, larger venues may have more specialised people creating and implementing each strategy.

All of the elements of the strategic marketing and strategic sales functions go hand in hand and are an integral part of what may be termed strategic venue management. This also includes all elements of operating the venue, from the back of house operation to the customer service function, all of which are key extensions of how the venue is marketed and sold. They play key roles in delivering the promises that take place during negotiations with potential clients.

The following chapter examines the strategic sales tasks of developing relationships with clients and entering into negotiations with them.

Palais des congrès de Montréal: "At the Centre of Everything" direct mail campaign

The venue

Located in the largest city in the province of Québec, Canada, the Palais des congrès de Montréal is a convention centre located in Montréal's downtown core.

The Palais was inaugurated in May 1983, and from 1999 to 2002, it underwent an expansion enabling it to double its capacity. The venue now features 200,000 sq ft (19,000 m²) of exhibition surface area, 65 meeting rooms and 18 loading docks, and is linked to 4,000 local hotel rooms by indoor walkways.

With its strikingly contemporary architecture featuring abundant natural light, the convention centre has hosted more than 5,500 events since 1983 and has earned a level of customer satisfaction close to 90%.

The mission of the Palais des congrès de Montréal is to attract and host conventions, exhibitions, consumer/trade shows, conferences, meetings and other events. Describing itself as 'a public institution with a commercial vocation', the Palais generates important economic and intellectual benefits for Québec and contributes to enhancing Montréal's international reputation as a first-class destination.

The Palais des congrès de Montréal, from Place Riopelle. Photo Stephan Poulin

The full height glass frontage fills the interior with coloured light. Photo courtesy Palais des congrès de Montréal

The challenge

Many Europe-based associations are far less familiar with Montréal as a conference destination than they are with European and US cities. Therefore, in order to inform international prospects about the destination and make them more likely to consider Montréal as a host city for their events, the Palais des congrès de Montréal wanted to build their awareness about their city and its many advantages.

The solution

A direct mail campaign was created, with the aim of positioning Montréal as a world-class destination for meetings and conventions, as well as positioning the Palais des congrès de Montréal as an industry leader among venues in North America. More specifically, the Palais des congrès had two objectives in deploying this direct mail campaign:

■   To inform international prospects about the layout of the city, the location of the Palais and its proximity to attractions and amenities;

- To demonstrate Montréal's signature creativity and originality, and present the Palais' unique selling proposition.

The strategy was to use the venue's sales team's presence at the EIBTM trade show in November 2012 to reach out to a targeted list of international prospects and invite them to visit the Palais des congrès de Montréal stand during this major annual exhibition in Barcelona. To achieve the objectives of the campaign, the material to be sent out in the direct marketing campaign had to be original, easy to personalize - and it had to clearly communicate the advantages of choosing Montréal and the Palais des congrès for an association conference.

The campaign

The innovative approach and creativity of this campaign was evident in the strong, iconic visual design of the marketing material and the high degree of personalization applied in the direct marketing.

The design and execution had to express the key notion of 'proximity' on multiple levels:

- Easy access to the destination: Montréal is easy for international travellers to access and is in close proximity to a large pool of potential attendees from the US and the rest of Canada.

- Walkable, compact downtown core: Montréal is easy to get around on foot, by car or public transit, putting a wide variety of gastronomic, entertainment and cultural experiences in close proximity to the Palais and most accommodation.

- Central location of the Palais: The Palais des congrès de Montréal is located in the heart of downtown Montréal, in close proximity to a vast array of amenities and attractions, from the hip and happening downtown sector to the historic atmosphere of Old Montréal and more.

- Close ties with key economic sectors: With its thriving health sciences, technology, academic, research and creative sectors, Montréal makes it easy for international associations to forge close ties with local communities in their field of activity. These close ties facilitate the planning and hosting of meetings and conventions in Montréal for Europe-based associations.

- Personalized, one-on-one service: The Palais team works closely with its clients to offer top-quality professional services, acting as a partner in their clients' success.

The campaign also had to reflect the Palais' unique selling proposition (USP) and values:

- Flexible spaces and ultra-modern facilities

- High-quality services, tailored to clients' needs

- A commitment to sustainable development, with a range of green meetings options.

The core of the design was a stylized map showing the streets of Montréal with a green "X" to indicate the location of the Palais in the heart of the city. The "X" design was integral to the concept as it communicated the idea of convergence, of many elements coming together at one location, both geographically and conceptually. Using marketing material based on this design, the marketing-communications team, working with its agency, Paprika, created a direct mail campaign that was complemented with advertisement placements and e-mail communications. The campaign was deployed intensively, starting in October 2012.

Personalization of the marketing messages

The goal of the campaign was to personalize the mailings according to the targeted client's sector of activity; therefore a great deal of time was invested in the planning stage to ensure intelligent choices. The marketing-communications team worked closely with the sales team to hand-pick the accounts that would receive the direct mail material. Health and sciences emerged quickly as sectors to target; but much dialogue and reflection went into grouping the remaining sectors. It was decided that 'knowledge' was the unifying concept to address associations in the fields of education, social sciences and politics. For clients outside of these sectors, 'creativity' was chosen as the common interest shared by these associations.

A series of seven small booklets was produced on specific themes: the Palais, the destination, proximity, and themes according to economic sectors (health and life sciences, knowledge, creativity, science and engineering).

Each booklet used bold text, images and graphics to provide information on an aspect of the city or the convention centre. Each mailing included four of the seven booklets: All clients received the Palais, the destination and the proximity booklets, while the fourth booklet varied according to the client's field of activity.

The four booklets were placed on the map of Montréal, with their covers forming a green "X" to mark the location of the Palais on the map, showing how it is indeed "At the Centre of Everything". The map then folded around the booklets like an origami puzzle game to form an envelope. This kept packaging to a minimum. All materials were 100% recyclable.

Some of the marketing materials produced by Paprika. Source: http://www.behance.net/gallery/Palais-des-congres-At-the-center-of-everything/9798499

Notebooks with stunning images and 'fast facts' about Montréal were also produced to give to prospects on-site at EIBTM. One batch was personalized for priority accounts the Palais team knew would be attending EIBTM; another batch was left blank as giveaways.

Because of limited time and budgets and the high degree of personalization required to deploy the concept, each step of the planning process was critical in the success of the campaign.

Using the venue's database to identify the target clientele

The Palais des congrès de Montréal's 'At the Centre of Everything' direct mail campaign targeted 350 prospects in international associations based in Europe. These were hand-picked by the sales and marketing teams based on:

- their potential to choose Montréal
- their conference rotation schedules, and
- their next open years.

A great deal of painstaking effort was focused on database analysis and the choice of clients' sectors of activity. This was a complex strategy in that it was impossible to create content specific to every single client's sector of activity, yet it was important to create a pertinent message for each client targeted. A total of 80% of the targeted accounts in the science and engineering, knowledge, and health and life sciences sectors received a highly customized message. The remaining 20% received a booklet showcasing Montréal's signature creativity, rather than an industry-specific message.

Complementary advertising support for the campaign

The complementary advertising placements in the *EIBTM Daily* magazines, *Meet and Travel Mag* and *Convention Source* reached an additional 58,200 readers before and during the show. For additional impact, the advertising placement in EIBTM had two components: a round sticker on the cover page of the magazine inviting readers to view the content on pages 8 and 9; and the double-page spread itself, featuring the "X" design boldly displayed on the right-hand panel.

Carefully timed deployment

Timing was a key to the success of the campaign; if the mailing went out to clients too early, it risked being diluted by the abundance of communications that clients receive before EIBTM. If sent too late, it risked arriving after clients departed for Barcelona.

Therefore, the campaign was deployed in a series of carefully timed phases:

- Early October: Production of all creative elements

- Late October: Mailing of the direct mail piece and delivery of print ads for the *EIBTM Daily* magazines, *Meet and Travel Mg* and *Convention Source*

- Early November: E-mail blasts from sales representatives to clients inviting them to visit the booth during EIBTM. The personalized and blank notebooks were also shipped to Barcelona in early November. Here, an unexpected development came into play: the notebook shipment was held at customs and was not released in time for EIBTM. The sales and marketing teams had to re-acquire the shipment and arrange for the notebooks to be mailed individually to clients after the event with personalized letters to say thank you, or "sorry we missed you".

- December: Post-event correspondence included e-mails and the notebooks mailed to EIBTM clients.

Because each mailing was personalized according to the client's sector of activity, a great deal of hands-on manipulation to assemble the pieces for mailing was required. The execution of the campaign necessitated great attention to detail.

Building on the success of the campaign

Positive reactions to the campaign from clients and peers and the strength of the creative approach inspired the Palais to adapt the campaign for its U.S. clientele in a second phase. The marketing-communications team and sales teams worked together to adjust the material to address the specific interests and concerns of U.S. clients when considering a host city.

Approximately 100 potential U.S. clients were targeted to receive the 'At the Centre of Everything' direct mail piece. The U.S. version of the campaign rolled out in two parts: the direct mail piece was sent in December 2012 before the PCMA Convening Leaders conference; then notebooks with personalized letters were mailed in January 2013, just after the conference. Seizing the opportunity to adapt the strategy for the U.S. market made efficient use of the budgets allocated for the original campaign, resulting in significant cost savings for the Palais.

Evaluating the campaign's success

The key lesson from this campaign was that a single, central message applied in a highly targeted way could provide a significant return on investment for the fraction of the cost of a traditional advertising campaign.

The objective was to build awareness and recall for the destination and the centre on the international association market with a limited budget and less than three months from concept to deployment. The total investment of $61,225 CAD (approximately €45,850 or £39,200) for the international direct mail campaign (including media) was a modest investment for a project of this scope and personalization.

The feedback received from clients at EIBTM was overwhelming positive. Prospects appreciated the originality of the design, the clarity of the information conveyed and the practicality of the approach. Many prospects contacted their sales representatives by e-mail after the show to compliment them on a job well done, which is unusual; it is rare that clients take the time to thank a marketer for a direct mail piece. One client, for example, wrote to say how much she appreciated the campaign, calling it, 'creative and fun and practical, too'.

While a direct correlation cannot be established between the campaign and specific sales, the fact that the Palais des congrès de Montréal attained its 2012-2013 sales objectives, coupled with anecdotal feedback received from clients, points to the clear success of the campaign.

Online resources

Sydney Convention and Exhibition Centre's blog topics: blog.scec.com.au/

London City Selection (LCS): www.londoncityselection.co.uk

Historic Conference Centres of Europe: www.hcce.com

International Association of Conference Centres: www.iacconline.org

Kellogg Conference Center: kelloggconferencehotel.com

Palais des congrès de Montréal: http://congresmtl.com/en/

Soaring Worldwide: www.soaringww.com

Online sources of further information

ActionCoach Business Coaching: 11 Ways to Double Your Customer Base in Four Weeks
www.actioncoach.com/white-papers

Directory Journal: How to Qualify Sales Leads and Prospects
www.dirjournal.com/guides/how-to-qualify-sales-leads-prospects/

Salesforce Marketing Cloud: How to Generate Leads with Social Media
www.salesforcemarketingcloud.com/resources/ebooks/
     how-to-generate-leads-with-social-media/

3 Developing Relationships with Clients

Customer relationship management systems

In order to turn qualified leads into actual revenue, it is essential for venue sales staff to efficiently manage those leads and develop relationships with them. Keeping track of where customers – and potential customers – currently are in the sales cycle is an important activity for every sales-driven business, and in order to do this, venues, just like any other businesses, need a formal, standardised way for staff to monitor their relationships with customers – especially when there is a team of people working in sales.

This is where a customer relationship management (CRM) system plays a central role. A reliable CRM system is vital to the successful functioning of any venue's sales activities. Such systems are usually built by the venue's management as a tool that allows their leads database to be efficiently managed through some form of software solution such as the Microsoft Windows package, GoldMine; or by using a web-based system such as SalesForce; or by simply using a system of shared Excel documents. More recently, open source CRM solutions have also appeared on the market – a group of software products, for which access to the source code is open, giving programmers the opportunity of making particular modifications to suit their company's unique business requirements. Open source CRM products are not free, but are often available at a significantly lower cost than commercial software, due to the differences in licensing agreements.

Whatever the technology used to drive the venue's CRM system, all relevant information about each lead in the database should be recorded there, as it will be useful at different stages of the sales process. In Chapter 2, we listed the basic information – to be captured on any prospect at the initial stage of being entered into the database. But for those leads qualified as being potential clients of the venue, all of the venue's dealings with the lead, as well as actions taken in connection with those dealings, should be systematically recorded. This will mean that any member of staff can log into the CRM system at any time and get access to this up-to-date information.

At a very basic level, the purpose of a sales CRM system is to organise the venue's sales process, improve communications between members of the sales team and managers, and free up staff time for sales tasks by improving efficiency. But CRM is not just the application of technology. It is an entire strategy which has as its objective a focus on customers' needs and behaviours in order to develop stronger relationships with them. One way in which this is achieved is through any effective CRM system's ability to develop more tailored communication channels between a venue and its prospects and clients.

Key account management

Another benefit offered by a CRM system is the effective management of key accounts. Key accounts are, fundamentally, those accounts (customers) who have been qualified as being of most value, actual and potential, to the venue. For example, the venue may have 10 accounts that, between them, are responsible for 60% of overall sales. These are known as key accounts, and they may be, for example, corporate clients, associations or agencies. Whatever segments of the meetings and events industry they represent, however, they are clearly of considerable strategic value to the venue. For that reason, their management is, by definition, among the most critically important of the venue's sales staff's activities.

Due to the significant returns which key accounts represent, the venue's sales force generally invests a significant amount of time and energy in establishing and nurturing these accounts. Larger venues may employ a key account manager (KAM) who is exclusively responsible for working with the venue's top 10 accounts or top five accounts, for example. For each of those accounts, the KAM should aim at establishing a close, personalised relationship in a way that he or she becomes a 'one-stop-shop' for the account – their designated contact within the venue.

For each key account, the KAM should develop explicit sales objectives and revenue targets. This can only be done if the KAM has extensive knowledge of the key account's business and its operations. For example, through their interactions with a key account, the KAM may learn that they hold 10 training events each year. Based on that knowledge, a target may be set, regarding how many out of the 10 events the venue can win. Half of them? All of them? Whatever the target set, this will give the KAM something measurable to aim for.

But, the management of key accounts should go beyond the mere setting of targets. An effective key account development plan would not only include sales objectives but also details of how the KAM will interact with the key account throughout a period of time, usually one year. For example:

☐ How many times in the year the KAM will meet with the key account for a review

- ☐ How many times in the year the key account will be invited into the venue for a refresher site-visit

- ☐ How and how often during the year the key account will be entertained, through, for instance, an invitation to lunch.

All of these interactions are opportunities for valuable face-to-face communication between the KAM and their key accounts. As such, they offer opportunities for the KAM not only to maintain the key account's value to the venue, but also to increase it. For example, one of the objectives in the key account development plan may be for the KAM to explore whether other departments, apart from the key account's own department, in that organisation hold events and, if they do, what types of events they are: training courses, awards ceremonies, hospitality events, and so on. A further objective might be to find out whether other branches of the key account's organisation – or their sister companies – may also require a venue for their events. Having obtained the details of other bookers in the key account's organisation, the KAM would then arrange meetings with them in order to qualify them and explore their needs. In this way, the key account's full potential as a client can be realised.

Negotiating with prospects

At any meeting between a representative of a venue and a prospect who is seeking a venue for a specific event, the negotiating process will inevitably get underway. The rest of this chapter examines the different elements of that process and ways in which venue representatives can most effectively win the confidence of prospects and convince them to become clients of their venue.

The ability to negotiate successfully is a key skill for any venue sales manager. Negotiations most often take place directly between the venue sales manager and a prospect representing the buyer organisation. But the negotiation may also involve an agency – the type of intermediary, working on behalf of the prospect, whose role is described in Chapter 4.

Negotiations between venues and prospects or agencies can take place in a number of different locations. But they usually occur when both parties are meeting face-to-face as a result of a planned event or appointment – for example, at a meetings industry exhibition (see Chapter 6), on the prospect's or agency's own premises, or during a site-visit to the venue itself.

■ Preparing for negotiations with prospects

The key to successful negotiations lies in thorough preparation, done well in advance of the meeting between both parties.

This begins with research into the prospect's organisation. As noted in the previous chapter, the Internet makes this easier than ever, as the organisation's own website will usually include useful information on its mission statement, its stakeholders, values, roles, and so on. The same website may also provide a profile of the person or people who will be representing the organisation.

Linkedin can also be a useful source of this information. Often, details of the event itself may be found on the organisation's website, particularly if it is an external meeting. If this includes information on where the event has been held in the past, then the venue sales manager may find it useful to contact that venue or those venues, to ask for information on issues such as how the event was run, the client's priorities, and any problems that may have occurred. Most venues will agree to sharing this kind of information with each other, particularly in the case of non-competing venues in different cities.

But it is important to look beyond what the organisation is saying about itself on its own website. What are others saying about it? For example, a review of the press coverage of the organisation may reveal that it is experiencing serious financial difficulties or is reeling from a public relations disaster. That kind of knowledge assists the venue sales manager in adopting a more understanding tone in their negotiations with the prospect.

Effective information-gathering of this type enables the venue sales manager to create a list of questions for the prospect and to prepare a set of points about the venue's strengths that they want to be sure to mention during the negotiation.

3

■   ## During the negotiation

Although checklists can be a useful tool for ensuring that no key points have been missed in the negotiation, it is important that the venue sales manager's approach should not look too rehearsed or over-programmed. Rather, encouraging the prospect to relax and talk about their organisation, their event, their challenges, etc., will usually produce most of the information the venue sales manager requires, without appearing to go through a pre-planned list of questions. It is important to aim for a natural conversation, not an interrogative style of questioning.

Negotiations that are effective for all parties always include a detailed discussion of the prospect's objectives and motivations for holding their event. These days, no-one has a meeting just for the sake of it. There is always a need for it, one or more compelling reasons for holding it. It is the venue sales manager's job to find out what those reasons are. However, this can be a challenge when, as sometimes happens, the prospect cannot clearly articulate what their objectives are. This is more likely to be the case in situations where the prospect is someone who only infrequently has to organise events – a secretary or a Human Resources Manager, for example, or someone organising an association or charity event on a voluntary basis. In such cases, the prospect may need to be prompted in their thinking about their event's objectives by the venue sales manager asking questions such as 'What is it that you are trying to get out of this event?'; 'How will you be able to tell to what extent your event has been successful?'

But it is important to remember that successful negotiations are an exchange of information, and that prospects will also have their own questions to ask. Again, the number and type of these questions will vary according to the level of experience of the person negotiating on behalf of the prospect. Experienced in-house meeting planners or agencies, for example, will usually come to the negotiation with a high level of understanding of what they are looking for. They may have already used the venue in question – in which case they will mainly be interested in hearing of any changes that have taken place (in terms of, for instance, the building's infrastructure or key staff changes) since they last held an event there. If not, they will have a list of specific, perhaps technical questions. Inexperienced, voluntary or occasional meeting planners may need more explanation and illustration of the extent to which the venue fits – or does not fit – their requirements. They may even need the venue sales manager's guidance in exploring the detailed requirements of the event they are planning.

Out-of-town meeting planners, whatever their level of experience, tend to have supplementary questions about local transport, accommodation, possible support from the Convention Bureau (see Chapter 4). In that case, the venue sales manager is likely to find themselves having to sell not only their venue space, but also the destination in which it is located.

3

While in most negotiations, the participants will be limited to a maximum of one or two sales staff from the venue and one or two representatives from the prospect side, in certain cases there may be a need for others to be present. For some types of event – technically-elaborate product launches or political meetings requiring high levels of security, for example – the prospect may wish to go into details about the venue's audio-visual facilities or the security arrangements. In those circumstances, the venue's Head Technician or Security Manager could be involved in the discussion. At times, even the General Manager of the venue can be brought into the discussion, if senior managers from the prospect organisation are present during the negotiations.

It is important throughout the negotiation that the venue's representative plays to the venue's strengths at all times, relating those wherever possible to the actual event under discussion. He or she can use examples of similar past events and clients' testimonies, focusing on why and how other clients have used the venue.

Agreeing a price

It should be clear from what has already been covered in this chapter that negotiating goes far beyond simply both parties agreeing on a price. Nevertheless, in most world regions it is the case that, particularly since the onset of the economic crisis, the issue of price has tended to assume greater prominence for most clients.

There are two elements to the price aspect of negotiations: how much the client is prepared to pay; and how much the venue will charge.

■ The prospect's budget

The prospect may or may not reveal their budget during a negotiation. When they decline to do so, the venue sales manager must use their powers of deduction to estimate what that budget might be. The type of prospect often provides an indication of the size of their budget. For example, generally speaking, the association segment tends to be more cost-conscious than the corporate sector. For associations, it is usually essential that they make a profit from the event – or at least break even. Even the government and corporate meetings sectors operate within constrained budgetary limits, with generally less funding at their disposal for events in time of economic downturn. They are also often cautious about appearing too lavish with public and company funds, in order to avoid criticism from their stakeholders.

In recent years, there has been a notable change in how the majority of clients manage their budgets. In the past, many of them failed to – or did not need to – take into account that, on top of the agreed price for the basic venue hire, there would be supplementary costs for items such as audio-visual facilities, parking and cloakroom services. Now, in more financially stringent times, more clients have a fixed, absolute budget, which means that there is no scope for them finding extra funds for additional services that they may not have anticipated having to pay for. This feature of negotiations will be returned to later in this chapter, when the issue of how venues can add value is discussed.

■ The venue's constraints

Those negotiating on behalf of their venues usually have some discretion in terms of the price they can accept from the prospect. However, they also understand that there are usually important parameters in terms of the minimum price they may accept for the hire of any particular meeting or event space. Knowledge of these parameters is essential. Venue managers need to be aware of the precise DDR (day delegate rate) that they need to achieve, based on a minimum number of delegates, in order to make a realistic profit. Beyond those parameters, there may be some flexibility in terms of rates, and these rates will be established as a result of the negotiation process.

But those negotiating on behalf of venues that are operating on a commercial basis need to be aware of the minimum level of income that they need to make as well as the actual profit margins on each space available for hire. It may be necessary to abandon a negotiation without an agreement, simply because the price being offered is too low

■ The price factor

The venue's price parameters – the minimum rates to be achieved for each meeting/event space – are usually set as a result of its yield management calculations. These calculations take into account not only the revenue that the venue needs to achieve to remain financially sustainable, but also what the market in general would be prepared to pay.

How do venues set rates for their meeting rooms? Many believe that such calculations are made using the manager's own intuition and experience, and these qualities can certainly play a part in the process. But there are other, more objective, examples of evidence that should inform these calculations:

- ☐ A key element is **competitor analysis**, which involves looking not only at similar venues but at all types of venues competing for business in the same market. It is not uncommon for venues to share this information among themselves; but in those situations where this is not the case, it may be possible to learn what competing venues' rates are by contacting them as a 'mystery shopper'. When businesses set their prices at a comparable level to their competitors, this is known as 'neutral pricing', and is commonly considered to be the safest pricing strategy. However, fixing rates by using neutral pricing alone has the major disadvantage that the company adopting this strategy may not be maximizing its profits, since the strategy is based purely on the market and not on the product or service being sold or hired.

- ☐ **Historical data** from the venue itself also constitutes an important factor in the calculation. How much has each meeting/event space earned in the past, on different days of the week, on different weeks of the year? Those rates can be a useful guide to what the venue can realistically earn from the same spaces in the future. Occupancy rates for each space are also vital statistics that must be taken into account in yield management calculations. Therefore, it is essential that venues create and maintain an efficient system for recording and storing these data.

☐ Other useful data that should be systematically recorded and used in yield management calculations are the **budgets mentioned by clients** when making enquiries. As was noted above, not all prospects volunteer this information; but when they do, it should be logged and shared internally, as a guide to how much that client had available to spend on venue hire for their event.

☐ Up-to-date and accurate **knowledge of market trends** can also provide a useful guide as to what clients are likely to be willing to pay. For example, macroeconomic conditions have a direct impact on factors such as business confidence, which in turn affects the price that organisations feel able to pay for the venues they use. An understanding of the current performance of specific market sectors can also be a valuable tool. For example, when preparing to negotiate with a prospect from the automotive sector, it would be helpful for the venue sales manager to be aware of how well that sector is currently performing – a 'feel-good' factor resulting from a booming car market may have consequences for how much that prospect is prepared to spend on a venue for their event.

Knowledge of the factors listed above enables the venue management to set rates that have a realistic chance of yielding satisfactory levels of profit and to answer questions such as: we have a meeting room with a 60% occupancy rate over the year at a rate of €700 per day; is it realistic to expect an annual occupancy rate of 85% if we lower the rate to €600 per day? Is there a local market for hiring our meeting rooms by the hour – short-notice, walk-in, ready-to-go?

However, the process of setting realistic targets for the yield from venues as a whole or for individual meeting rooms within a venue has become more complex in recent years. As stated above, prices were traditionally based, partly at least, on historic booking patterns – the levels of demand for meetings facilities in the venue on specific days of specific weeks over the previous few years. But over recent years, a growing number of venues are finding that their booking patterns and lead times have changed and, as a result, they can no longer rely on past booking behaviours as a guide to the future. Clients are booking later and appear to be more willing to hold their events on what were traditionally, for venues, the quieter days (Mondays and Fridays) and months in order to negotiate a cheaper rate. This has meant that many venues have had to rethink their yield management policies in order to take into account these new booking patterns.

In all negotiations on price, it is a sound policy for the venue representative to be transparent and honest with the prospect. It can often be appropriate to explain to prospects the reasons why the venue needs to charge the prices being asked for room hire: for example, the venue has overheads and other costs; and ultimately, perhaps as may be the case for the prospect, is in business to make a profit for shareholders; or, in the case of unique venues based in museums or other cultural centres, to support the cultural activities of those centres.

Demonstrating and adding value

In any negotiation, the temptation to cut prices in order to win business is never entirely absent, particularly in the case of inexperienced sales staff. But in the management literature it is axiomatic that price cutting can rarely be justified as a tactic. Price cuts hurt profit margins, reduce the quality of service levels and decrease employee morale. The most unfortunate result may be a price war, when competitors retaliate in an attempt to maintain market share. Price wars, the 'race to the bottom', can confuse regular customers, who may begin to wonder if they are receiving the same quality of service from suppliers that have noticeably cut their prices. Also, when venues drastically cut their prices to fill their spaces, this inevitably makes it difficult for them to raise prices again, as returning clients will expect to pay similarly discounted rates. Indeed, most clients understand that it is in their best interests to pay higher prices if this means that the services they seek can be reliably delivered on a long-term basis. They see that if a venue they regularly use goes out of business due to price cutting, or even simply deteriorates due to lack of investment in maintenance or staff training, then they need to take the risk of taking their business elsewhere.

In the meetings and events market, most buyers tend to be value-oriented, in the sense that they will choose higher value services, if they perceive genuine value, or can be made to understand that by using a particular venue rather than its competitors they will be more likely to achieve the objectives for their event. Therefore, in preference to price-cutting, a much more effective approach for venue sales managers in negotiations is to demonstrate or add value, thereby shifting the focus from price to questions of value.

For example, at a time when a growing number of clients have a fixed budget for their events, with no scope for paying for 'extras', it can be attractive for them if, during the negotiation process, facilities such as audio-visual or cloakroom services can be added to the overall package at no extra cost – in particular if competing venues are charging extra for these. Adding value in this way can often be done at negligible cost to the venue, since such facilities are usually already in place.

In looking for ways of adding value to clients' events, venue managers should be as innovative as possible, and make full use what the venue can offer at no-cost or low-cost. For example, the historic venue, Ironmongers Hall, situated in Central London offers a historical tour of the building as part of the package.

Another way of the venue adding demonstrable value would be by offering to help with the actual marketing of the client's event. Association conferences or charity events for example generally welcome any assistance with what is known as 'attendance-building' – providing publicity for the event that helps boost the numbers of participants attending. Figure 3.1 lists some of the most effective ways in which venues can assist with the marketing of the events they host.

1. List your event on their website

Straightforward and effortless, a spot on your venue's homepage could enable your event to be seen by thousands of people. What's more, links from other websites can be really beneficial for search engine optimisation (SEO), meaning your own website could become more visible as a result too.

2. Have a whole page on their site

Better than just listing it, why not have a dedicated page on their website that links directly to information that your delegates need to know (how to get to there, nearby accommodation, etc.)?

3. Free online advertising

Most venues have plenty of space on their sites that could be used for advertising. Some use that space to promote their own services, and there is no reason why it can't be used to promote your events too.

4. Become the news

Almost every venue has a 'latest news' section on their site, and that is the perfect place to find your press releases.

5. Harness the power of Twitter

Most venues will have hundreds, if not thousands, of followers on Twitter; and tapping into them is as easy as 140 characters. Twitter can be a very powerful tool for promoting events, and the more profiles you have working for you, the more potential there is for your audience to grow exponentially.

6. Take advantage of other social media

Your venue will no doubt be using a plethora of other social media tools, so why not ask them to talk about your event across them all?

7. Increase coverage through public relations

A good venue is likely to have good PR channels, which help your event get more coverage than it might otherwise, so why not share all your latest releases with them.

8. Exploit digital signage and other on-site advertising

Your venue could have hundreds, thousands, or even millions of delegates passing through their doors; meaning a well-placed advert could make a real difference.

9. Get help with your marketing strategy

A venue is already helping to plan all the other elements of the event, and they are likely to have marketing specialists in their team, so why not ask them for help with you marketing strategy too?

Figure 3.1: Nine ways a venue can help you promote events for free. Source: eventistry.net

The Museum of Brands, Packaging and Advertising, London

Adding value to clients' events by offering a quiz as an add-on team-building exercise.

The venue

The Museum of Brands can be classified as an unusual venue. Its primary function is to present to the public its permanent display of over 12,000 branded items spanning 150 years of consumer culture. These items, covering all aspects of daily life from toys, magazines and technology to travel, souvenirs and fashion from the Victorian era to the present day, formed the private collection of Robert Opie, a brand and consumer historian, who is now the museum's director. Opened in 2005 in London's Notting Hill area, the museum offers visitors an insight into brand evolution and brand dynamics.

The museum's dedicated conference room looks out over a picturesque mews and is used for a range of different events, from innovation sessions and workshops to lunches. It can accommodate up to 70 attendees theatre-style, 35 cabaret or 24 boardroom.

The museum itself is available for the hosting of events outside the times when it is open to the public (Tuesdays - Saturdays, 10.00 -18.00; Sundays, 11.00 -17.00). With the museum's collection of exhibits as a backdrop, it can host dinners for up to 55 guests or drinks receptions/product launches/parties for up to 120 guests.

The clients

The venue successfully builds upon its unique collection of brands to win meetings and events. Advertising itself as 'The world's only brand heritage venue' (http://www. museumofbrands.com), the museum positions itself as 'an ideal choice for companies who regard branding and design as an integral part of their business' (ibid). As a result, many of the venue's clients include actual brand owners, retailers, creative agencies, marketers and advertisers. Some corporate clients use the venue because it offers their attendees the opportunity to discover the history of their own company brand during the event. The Museum of Brands is also frequently used by companies for their product launches and press launches, when the opportunity to visit the collection acts as an additional attraction for those who are invited.

The Quiz

The initiative of offering a quiz as an add-on activity for attendees was launched in February 2013, after the idea was generated at one of the museum's internal monthly marketing meetings. There were four main objectives for this:

- To entertain and to teach attendees about the museum's collection.

- To act as a team-building exercise.

- To provide a link, in the attendees' minds, between the museum's dual roles as a cultural attraction and a venue.

- To have something new to offer clients who have previously used the venue.

The quiz is offered to all of the venue's clients, and, for those who accept it, attendees are put into groups and given a list of questions (see Figure 3.2). The quiz can be used as a lunchtime activity or at the end of the day. Or, for evening events, it can be run before dinner, as an ice-breaker.

A: Guess the date that these brands were launched in.

1. In which year was Nescafe instant coffee launched in the UK? 1929 1939 1949

2. When did the Mars bar arrive in the UK? 1932 1948 1957

3. Which year was the breakfast cereal Frosties launched in the UK? 1954 1964 1974

4. When was Pot Noodle launched in the UK? 1971 1975 1978

5. When did Watneys Party Seven appear in the UK? 1963 1968 1972

B: Brand names are a critical part of the marketing world; see how many you can identify…

1. TV commercials were first shown in Britain in 1955. Which brand was the first?

_____

2. Which classic brand was launched in 1886 as a popular fortifying hot beverage and, in the 1920s had the slogan 'prevents that sinking feeling'?

_____

3. For many years it was called Liebigs Extract of Meat and arrived as a cube in 1910. What was the snappier name that gave new life to this brand?

_____

4. Name the Australian shoe shine brand that came to Britain in 1913. Clue: the inventor's wife came from New Zealand.

_____

5. Which popular tea brand was launched in the 1930s under the name Pre-Gestee?

_____

C: Fill in the blanks with the brand name that famously uses the following slogans…

1. 'Ten to one it's _____ time'

2. 'Exceedingly good cakes' _____

3. 'A glass and a half ' _____

4. *'Someone's Mum doesn't know what someone's Mum ought to know. That* _____
washes whiter'

5. *'Probably the best beer in the world'* _____

Figure 3.2: The quiz questions.

In order to obtain to answers to these questions, the attendees have to move through the museum's collection, studying the exhibits, although the answers to some of the questions rely on the attendees' personal knowledge of brands and branding. On average, the quiz takes 30 minutes to complete.

When the event organiser decides to offer a prize to the winning team, the museum offers items from its gift shop at a discounted rate, so that attendees have a souvenir of the museum (all items in the gift-shop are linked to the museum's collection). For the venue, this brings the added bonus of generating revenue for the retail department of the museum.

Results

The venue systematically collects feedback from clients, on how useful they found the quiz, for their events. This feedback is collected via email, and forms one of the subjects included in a short questionnaire that is sent to organisers a week after their event. Other aspects covered in the feedback questionnaire include service, catering and facilities.

In the first few months following the launch, approximately 30-35% of the venue's clients took up the offer of running the quiz for the attendees at their events. The principal factor preventing this proportion from being higher was found to be the limitations on the time available for this activity. Many events are running to a very full schedule that does not allow time for add-on attendee activities like the quiz.

All feedback returned within the first few months of the museum offering this quiz reported a 100% satisfaction rate both in terms of the length of the quiz and the level of difficulty of the questions.

Providing solutions

In all kinds of industries, there is currently a move away from sales-people acting as mere 'order-takers' towards them assuming the role of 'solution providers' or 'solution creators'. And the venue sector is no exception. 'Order-takers' focus on the product or service they are trying to sell, rather than what their prospects are trying to achieve. They may be very well-informed about the features and benefits of their product, but their perspective is solely from their own, supplier, side of the buyer-supplier relationship. 'Solution providers', on the other hand, focus on the outcomes and results that the customer will achieve if they use the product or service in question. In this way, they create value for their clients by giving them ideas for opportunities to improve their businesses. And this approach is particularly effective when negotiations appear to hit an obstacle.

Some of the most effective sales managers in venues attribute their success to the way they work together with prospects to find mutually-beneficial solutions to problems identified during negotiations. In this sense, they are acting less as salespeople representing one side of the buyer-supplier relationship and more as partners of the prospect, working to find solutions that work for all stakeholders.

For example, if the cost of the room hire is an obstacle to an agreement being reached with a client on a limited budget, the venue sales manager can explore whether the event's dates are really fixed, or whether the client be persuaded to consider dates that are less expensive. Or can the price be reduced by cutting back on the length of time the client needs to use the venue for? Do they really need all of the rooms they have requested for all of the time they have requested? Do they need as much set-up time in advance of their event? Can the venue manager suggest more effective use of the venue's facilities than that proposed by the prospect? (After all, the venue manager has a better understanding of the venue's potential, having seen the ways in which many other clients have used the venue's facilities). Perhaps the venue would accept a lower rate for the meeting room if the client agreed to a multi-year deal – obtaining a discount in return for booking the same venue over the following three years, for example. Or the venue might agree to freeze the rate over the following three years if the client makes a booking for three annual events, for example. Such multi-year deals can be attractive to the venue because they provide the security of repeat-business over an extended period of time.

An alternative financial model might even take the form of profit-sharing between the venue and the client, a formula that has been known to work well in the case of events for which registrations are sold – for example association events or commercial conferences that generate revenue through delegate fees. The venue may offer a reduced room rate based on a lower minimum number than it would generally accept for the meeting space, on the understanding that if the client achieves over the minimum number, either the venue charges more for the room or shares the additional revenue earned from the tickets sold above the minimum number. Under this financial model, if the client sells tickets at levels considerably over the agreed minimum, they as well as the venue benefit. This type of agreement represents an attractive form of risk-sharing between the venue and its client.

Finally, it is worthy of note that in the case of those venues where profits go to charitable causes or to support the arts for example, this can be emphasised during negotiations as a unique selling point. This aspect of the venue's structure may help convince the prospect to agree on a proposed price, as many organisations are more comfortable spending money when they know that some of it will go to worthy causes. In this way, their outlay on hiring a venue may then be regarded as part of their Corporate Social Responsibility (CSR) policy. In fact the venues' own CSR credentials could in themselves well be instrumental in closing the deal as many companies now have their own policies to which they need to adhere. Chapter 7 explores in more detail how venues can demonstrate their commitment to the environment.

■ Making the offer more flexible

One of the most common complaints against venues from meetings and events planners is the inflexible nature of the product or service on offer – for example, the venue's catering and beverage packages being entirely non-negotiable. Solution providers negotiating on behalf of the venue understand that, in this example, it can be attractive to the prospect if the venue is prepared to produce a bespoke menu that more closely suits their budget or their attendees' requirements. For example, although venues' fixed published menus may suit many events organisers' requirements, on occasion some flexibility and imagination may be required in order to adapt to a client's budget. For example, would the venue agree to offering one less coffee break for the cost-conscious meeting planner; or the ability to combine items from different menus?

On the other hand, in the case of negotiations with prospects on more lavish budgets, the food and beverage element of the package could provide an up-selling opportunity in the form, for example, of an upgrade to bacon sandwiches with morning coffee instead of biscuits; or a bespoke menu specifically themed to the topic of their event.

Flexibility is a key element of successful negotiations, and that is why negotiating on behalf of a venue can never be simply a case of reading from a set of scripted rules. By exploring alternatives in ways such as those outlined above and demonstrating flexibility the venue sales manager is seen to be working with the client to reach a satisfactory solution, and this reinforces the all-important sense of partnership.

Dealing with objections

Regardless of how outstanding a venue may be and how appropriate to the prospect's needs, prospects will almost always raise objections and express doubts during the negotiation process. In selling, one definition of an objection is 'a reason given by the prospective customer why they are not ready to buy your product or service.' In the context of venue sales, objections might include, for example:

- ☐ The conference centre is very large. Our delegates will have problems finding their way around and we'll lose valuable time because of that

- ☐ Transport links to the venue are lacking

- ☐ The location is a problem due to a lack of local amenities such as accommodation

- ☐ There is a lack of breakout space

- ☐ There is insufficient natural daylight

- ☐ There is no outdoor space

Successfully concluding a sale depends upon the venue sales manager's ability to anticipate and handle objections such as these. In order to do this, it is crucial that the person negotiating on behalf of the venue is fully aware of its limitations and previous objections that have been raised, and has convincing solutions available to address them.

Inexperienced sales people can sometimes dread objections, but in fact they are to be welcomed as they demonstrate that the prospect is interested in getting further information on the product. It is important to let the prospect express objections freely and fully. It is often worth repeating the objection back to the prospect, to make sure that it has been properly understood. Then the venue sales manager should acknowledge the objection (even if it is unfounded!), using a phrase such as 'I can see why you think that, because other meeting planners have expressed the same concern …' This shows respect for the point raised by the prospect, creates a degree of empathy, and is far preferable to immediately contradicting the prospect and risking creating a conflictual tone to the discussion.

Next, the sales manager should provide their solution to the objection, using practical examples of what the venue has done for past clients – and even testimonials if possible. For instance: 'I can see why you think that, because other meeting planners have expressed the same concern … but when they saw how we used signposting and staff to guide attendees around the venue, they realized that this wouldn't be an obstacle to a successful event'.

Answering objections is easier for experienced sales staff, as prospects tend to express the same objections during negotiations and sales managers become familiar with them and have the solutions ready.

However, there is a category of objections that presents more of a challenge for any sales manager: these are often known as 'liabilities' and they can be contrasted with the other category of objections, 'misunderstandings'. Misunderstandings are, as the name suggests, misconceptions about the product that are fairly effortlessly dealt with, as in the example above, about signposting. Liabilities, however, are major obstacles to agreement, and are often in fact deal-breakers. For example, if the prospect is looking for a hotel venue with a spa and golf course as essential elements of the package, this requirement represents a major liability to any venue lacking one or both of these facilities. Or if the prospect is set upon the idea of using a rural venue, to avoid the attendees being distracted by city-centre attractions, this will constitute an insuperable liability for any urban venue. Fortunately for sales managers, the vast majority of objections are misunderstandings for which solutions can be proposed without much difficulty.

Walking away – unsuccessful negotiations

Faced with liabilities of the type mentioned above, the prospect and sales manager may have no alternative but to terminate the negotiation without an agreement being reached. This is often the case when there is simply a mis-match between the prospect's requirements and the venue's features. Or it may be that no price that is acceptable to both sides can be found. It may even be that the prospect decides to take their business to a competing venue, because – all other things being equal (price, facilities, etc.) – they are risk-averse and simply prefer to deal with the person they already know in that other venue. The power of already being familiar to clients from hosting past events of theirs cannot be over-estimated.

But generally, the most common reason for negotiations failing is that the sales manager has not asked the appropriate questions and/or has not proposed effective solutions. This chapter has suggested ways in which negotiations can be concluded to the satisfaction of both sides.

Further reading

Holden, R K and Burton M R (2008) *Pricing with Confidence: 10 ways to stop leaving money on the table*, John Wiley & Sons, Hoboken, NJ

Friedman, D D (1990) *Price Theory: An Intermediate Text*, South-Western Publishing Co., Cincinnati, OH

Lewicki R J and Hiam A (2006) *Mastering Business Negotiation – A working guide to making deals and resolving conflict*, Jossey-Bass, San Francisco, CA

Mohammmed R (2005) *The Art of Pricing: How to find the hidden profits to grow your business*, Crown Publishing Group, NY

Nagle, T T, Hogan J E, Zale, J (2011) *The Strategy and Tactics of Pricing*, Prentice Hall, NJ

Raiffa H (1982) *The Art and Science of Negotiation*, Harvard University Press, Cambridge

Van Boven L and Thompson L (2003) 'A look into the mind of the negotiator: mental models in negotiation' in *Group Process Intergroup Relations* **6**(4): 387–404

Online sources of further information

Harvard Business Review Blog Network: How to Succeed at Key Account
Management, by Lynette Ryals

http://blogs.hbr.org/2012/07/how-to-succeed-at-key-account/

International Congress and Convention Association (ICCA): Negotiating with
hotels

www.iccaworld.com/cdps/cditem.cfm?nid=4084

International Congress and Convention Association (ICCA): Contracting with
major congress & convention venues

www.iccaworld.com/cdps/cditem.cfm?nid=5088

3

4 Working with Intermediaries

The role of intermediaries

Intermediaries are third parties who play a valuable role in the sales process by bringing buyers and sellers together and acting as a conduit between those two trading partners. Their role in any market system is best understood as adding value by bridging the various types of 'separations' or 'discrepancies' that can prevent contacts being made between suppliers of goods or services and their potential clients.

These market separations, or what McInnes (1964) called 'gaps', need to be resolved if buyers and sellers are to be satisfied. Time, information and space are among the types of market separations that may prevent suppliers from selling their goods or services to end users. In terms of the market for manufacturers' goods, Shaw (2013) illustrates these using the following examples:

- ❑ Manufacturers exist in a limited number of locations, but households are scattered across the landscape (spacial discrepancy)

- ❑ Manufacturers have a supply and households have a demand, but each party has to know the other exists and where to find them (information discrepancy)

- ❑ Manufacturers produce some goods seasonally, such as oranges, but households want these products all year around, while others produce products all year around, such as Christmas trees and bulbs, but households want them seasonally (time discrepancy).

These discrepancies, separations or gaps between buyers and sellers provide the opportunity for market activity to be performed by middlemen or intermediaries. By acting as a bridge between supply and demand, the role of the intermediary can be crucial to the business relationship. Especially in cases where the seller and the buyer do not have direct contact with each other, the intermediary is in a position to be able to influence the character of the business relationship. In this sense, the other two parties are dependent upon the intermediary's performance.

In the meetings and events market, there exist various types of intermediaries that can be effective in linking venues with potential customers. From the perspective of the venues, these intermediaries may be regarded as an extension of their own sales force. In this chapter, the roles of the two most important intermediaries for venues are examined: agencies and convention and visitor bureaus.

Types of agencies

While many large associations, organisations and corporations have their own, in-house, events department with responsibility for organising meetings and finding suitable venues for them, others choose to outsource these functions to external agencies – because, for example, the company is too small or their meetings and events are too infrequent too justify having a permanent in-house events department, or simply because the company finds that using the services of an external agency is a more cost effective and time saving solution. The growing role of procurement in the corporate meetings and events purchasing process has also increased the emphasis on companies' use of agencies.

In the past few years, corporate procurement departments have become increasingly involved in the process of choosing suppliers and venues for their companies' meetings and events. As a result, a growing number of companies now have to use the services of a nominated agency, which has gone through the procurement process, when selecting venues.

The relationship between client and agency may take the form of a 'preferred' agreement between the client and one sole agency, or through the client working with a selection of agencies. Some clients, for example, may use one company to find the venue, and hire another agency to take care of the actual production of their event. In any case, agencies' clients usually remain responsible for the actual content of their meetings (overall themes, presentation topics, choice of speakers), while the agencies themselves handle some or all of the other details, including finding venues, negotiating contracts and taking care of all aspects of on-site meeting management. (There are however a growing number of agencies who work with corporates in a strategic way to plan their overall event strategy, and such agencies' responsibility does extend to planning the actual content).

From the perspective of venues, therefore, agencies are key intermediaries, linking their properties with potential users and acting as a valuable additional selling arm.

Agencies may be classified according to the range of different services they provide. While many limit themselves to venue placement – identifying suitable venues for their clients' events – others also offer a more comprehensive array of services such as hotel accommodation booking, event management, and delegate registration.

Those providing venue placement services only are often known as venue finders or venue finding agencies; while those agencies undertaking a wider range of logistical services in connection with their clients' events may use titles such as 'events management agencies', 'association management companies', 'independent meeting planners' or 'professional conference organisers' (PCOs). When agencies, in addition, offer creative, technology-based solutions to enhance the appearance of their clients' events, they often use the title, 'events production companies'. Events production companies' services may include anything from set design and construction and the training of speakers to advising on the strategic aspect of a conference.

Agencies can be run by one person, working from their own home; or they can be large organisations working on the international scale. Some agencies may specialise in certain types of events, for example, medical conferences, government events or automotive events. Large agencies may have different teams with different specialisations and expertise in those particular fields. Other agencies specialise in planning and running events for the association segment of the meetings market (association management companies or PCOs).

From their clients' perspective, the principal value of agencies in the venue selection process lies in their ability to use their knowledge of venues in order to save valuable time for their clients, who simply provide them with a list of criteria (for example, the dates of the event, number of participants, whether accommodation is required, as well as any special requirements such as a golf course or a spa).

The agency then matches the client's requirements with the venues they have on their database, and provides the client with a shortlist of suitable venues. They may refine their search by asking their client the kind of questions that venues themselves use in order to work effectively with clients, such as 'What are the event's objectives?' or 'What is the profile of the group that will be attending the event?' The answers to questions such as these are also of particular help to those agencies who go as far as advising their clients on their strategic use of meetings and their content.

Agencies get their knowledge of venues from a range of sources including the meetings industry press, attendance at meetings industry trade shows and the internet. They need to constantly familiarise themselves with new venues and changes to existing venues on their databases, so that their knowledge is always up-to-date.

Agencies' remuneration

In terms of how agencies are remunerated, while many venue placement services are paid commission by the venues they recommend, others, including those agencies that undertake a wider range of tasks on behalf of their clients can be remunerated for their services in a number of ways. A recent survey by the Event Leadership Institute (Hatch, 2013) identified five types of pricing for agencies' services: mark-ups, commissions, percentage of budget, hourly/daily fee, and flat fee. Mark-ups and commissions were found to be the least popular pricing option, for both agencies and their clients. It is likely that the low use of these two fee models is evidence of the growing trend toward transparency in pricing. With non-disclosed models (mark-ups and commissions), the amount the agency is paid is not always transparent to the client, unless of course the agency chooses to make it so.

It is sometimes argued that the commission model itself is flawed, because, in theory an agency could be motivated to drive up their client's expenditure on the hire of a venue for their event, so that the agency can earn a higher commission. However, in reality, there is little evidence of such practices because one of the main arguments used by agencies in promoting their services to clients is that they can (and usually do) negotiate better rates with venues.

In the Event Leadership Institute survey, payment to agencies as a percentage of the overall budget for the event in question was found to be only slightly more popular than mark-ups and commissions as a fee system. The percentage charged ranged from 10 percent to 30 percent of the budget, with the average being 18 percent.

The system whereby agencies are remunerated in the form of an hourly rate or daily fees was found to be used 'most of the time' or 'always' by 23 percent of the survey respondents, with the majority of them charging less than US$100 per hour.

But in the same survey, it was clear that agencies and their clients preferred a flat fee approach to pricing by a fairly wide margin—23 percent used it 'always', 30 percent 'most of the time', 34 percent 'sometimes', and only 12 percent 'never'. However, the report noted that "any pricing method is acceptable if it's agreed to by both the client and the planner." In many cases, more than one pricing model may be used on a given project. For example, the report notes, "a planner may be paid for the site-selection portion of their scope of work via a commission, and a flat fee for the logistics and execution of the program."

How venues can work effectively with agencies

It is very advantageous for venues to maintain positive relationships with agencies, as those intermediaries have the potential to find business on the venue's behalf. It is important for venue managers therefore to manage their relationship with agencies in a mutually beneficial way.

Effective communication between the venue, the agency and the client is essential to the smooth running of the process. Supportive, professional agencies act as efficient communication conduits between venues and their clients, smoothing the sales process to the benefit of all parties. Such agencies actively sell the benefits of the venue to their clients, rather than simply communicating to them the price of venue hire.

In order to inform agency staff about their venue's benefits and features, venue sales managers should make regular appointments with agencies, to present their venue to them in exactly the same way that they would present it directly to prospects. Those appointments could be in the agencies' own offices, or they could take the form of a show-round at the venue itself. This represents an effective investment on the part of the venue staff, as agencies can only recommend the venue in an appropriate manner if they have up-to-date knowledge of how the venue can truly serve their clients' needs.

Working with agents can be of considerable benefit to venues, on condition that both parties are working together, taking fully into account what the end-client is looking for. The challenge for venue managers in this supplier-intermediary-buyer chain is that they usually have no initial direct contact with the end-client. That means that they are dependent upon the agency to find out what the client needs from the venue in order to make their event a success. With an intermediary standing between the venue and the end-client, the venue manager is usually unable to directly ask the types of qualifying questions that were described in Chapter 3. Professional, experienced agencies are those that understand the client's events and choose venues based on the actual brief and what the client is trying to achieve. But inexperienced or ineffectual agencies who fail to ask appropriate questions and explore their clients' needs fully can become an obstacle to a venue's success, rather than its supportive partner.

Some agencies may not even reveal who their client or prospect is. This can prove to be a challenge for venues which have a policy of refusing to hold space without knowing who the client is – usually to avoid clashes: for example, hosting events run by two competing financial institutions in the same venue on the same day.

Naturally, one important aspect of the relationship between venues and agencies is financial – particularly in those cases where the agency is charging commission for bringing business to the venue. Different remuneration models are possible. For example:

☐ Many venues have a preferred list of some agencies to whom they pay higher levels of commission (15% instead of 10%, for instance) in return for being considered for those agencies' business before any other venues.

☐ There is also the system of 'over-ride agreements' (commonly used by hotels) whereby if the agency succeeds in placing a pre-agreed amount of business with the venue, the venue will give them a bonus as a financial incentive to bring them clients.

☐ Venues may operate a system of contracted rates/ preferred rates with some agencies, offering them lower DDRs in return for those agencies bringing the venues a minimum amount of business over the year. The advantage of this system for the agency is that their clients are more likely to book with them, because they are getting a lower price through them than through other agencies with no contracted/preferred rates.

Closely linked to financial dealings between venues and agencies are the various ethical issues that can arise in the venue booking process, when a third party is involved.

For example, the situation can arise where, because the client has put out its event to multiple agencies, a venue receives the same enquiry from different agencies. Transparency should be the rule in such cases, with the venue making it known to the second agency that it has already had this enquiry from another agency. In terms of which agency earns the commission, the obvious answer is that it is paid to whichever agency is the first to confirm the booking.

The situation can also arise whereby an agency comes to the venue with an enquiry for a client, but then the same client comes to the venue directly. The venue must then decide whether or not to inform the agency; and whether or not to pay them their fee. In such a situation, most venues would proceed on the basis that if the client was introduced to them by the agency, it would be only fair to remunerate them for that – an effective way of keeping the relationship with the agency positive.

However, in the case of repeat business (for example, a client's annual conferences) when the client was initially introduced to the venue by an agency but subsequently came directly to the venue, it may be that no fee is paid to the agency after the initial commission, as the agency has thereafter been by-passed by their client. But even in these circumstances a venue may decide to pay a commission (or a reduced commission) if it is trying to build a positive relationship with the agency. Most venues make this decision on a case-by-case basis.

As a general rule, relationships between venues and agencies (as between venues and clients) work best in an atmosphere of openness and transparency. From the perspective of venues, agencies are an effective way of winning business, because agencies are already in contact with clients in need of a venue, which means that there is no need for the venue to go looking for them. When agencies work in partnership with the venue, they represent a valuable source of bookings and a powerful extension of the venue's own sales team. From the agencies' perspective, they have their own reputation to protect as well as the best interests of their clients to look after.

Jacqui Kavanagh, Managing Director of the UK-based agency Trinity Event Solutions gives the agency's viewpoint:

> When we as agents contact a venue, we are not just looking for space. We are looking for a venue that is going to ensure the success of our client's event, from the initial phone call where we assess the professionalism and knowledge of the venue sales person. We often test their ability to make decisions that will support our client on such issues as price and contract terms. What precisely do we want from the venue?

- From the venue's proposal for our client's event, we want to see if the brief has been not just understood but really grasped and then added to with additional venue knowledge that can really bring something extra to the option.

- We want our client's site visit to be taken very seriously and planned to military precision.

- We want to feel our client is in safe hands and we want feedback.

- We want the whole relationship to be one of trust and openness whether it's on additional costs, commissions or cancellations – and we want this to be consistent.

Finally, from the client's perspective, it is clear that this three-party system works best when the client sees that the venue and the agency are working together as one to help deliver a fully successful event.

4

The 'Chudbus' Summer Holiday Tour

Using an innovative and unique roadshow experience to present the Sundial Group of venues to Hotel Booking Agents

The venue

The Sundial Group (www.sundialgroup.com) is a family-run, hospitality group which owns and runs three country house venues in England: Barnett Hill in Surrey, Highgate House in Northamptonshire and Woodside in Warwickshire, all of which provide dedicated meeting and training environments.

Our principal market sector is business meetings and management training, and our core clients are national and multinational organisations.

The challenge

In the UK, Hotel Booking Agents (HBAs) are intermediaries that specialise in the procurement of accommodation, conference and event facilities and services on behalf of their clients.

We became aware that our core clients - national and multinational organisations - were increasingly procuring venues for their meetings through HBAs. However, we also recognised that HBAs deal mostly with larger hotel brands where the number of venues and geographic spread better fits most large organisations' procurement policies. For that reason, it was often more difficult, in our experience for small suppliers like ourselves to gain access to the booking teams of the big HBAs.

The Summer Holiday roadshow was our solution to this challenge.

The roadshow's objectives

The objective of our roadshow was to raise HBAs' awareness of Sundial's brand, our venues, unique character, history and values, in order to increase the value of business that we get from them.

The principles of our strategy for the roadshow were:

- People do business with those they connect with and trust.

- Brands are memorable if they have a unique personality and clearly established points of difference.

- Meeting over a meal and a remarkable story is memorable

- 'Straight from the horse's mouth' lends authenticity and is effective in creating trust.

We wanted to connect on a personal level with those who book venues and show them that not all conference centres are the same. All HBAs receive an overwhelming number of presentations from all types of venues each year, so in order for ours to stand out from the others, we felt that it was critical to be engaging, memorable, informative and to establish the key points of difference between the Sundial brand and other venues.

We had past experience of hosting fam-trips for small groups of HBAs, and these proved that once greater awareness and trust were established we got more business from the fam-trip participants, whose improved knowledge of our product also resulted in a higher proportion of RFPs (initial enquiries) becoming bookings and more of those being confirmed.

We wanted a memorable and cost effective way of getting the same results from a larger audience, so we created the Summer Holiday roadshow as a means of achieving the benefits of the fam-trip experience without HBAs having to take valuable time away from their desks to visit our venues in person. In financial terms, our objective was to increase by £100,000 the revenue that we earn from HBAs to and to increase the proportion of initial enquiries leading to successful bookings by 10%.

The planning process

Planning began in the winter before the roadshow, when our Agency Sales Manager, Mia Butler, secured presentation appointments with HBAs significantly in excess of those normally offered to a supplier of our size, by creating interest and excitement through the sheer creativity of our roadshow campaign.

Resources were largely sourced internally, resulting in a budget of £10,000 covering an allocation for refurbishment of the vehicle used for the roadshow, al-fresco paella equipment, fuel costs, marketing and consumables such as the food and drink for our guests as well as gifts such as our own sticks of seaside rock with 'Sundial Group' written through them – in keeping with the summer holiday theme.

A shared appointments diary was created on the Sundial intranet to coordinate the team. Each day of the roadshow campaign required meticulous attention to the detail of budget, timings, provisions and logistics. We wanted every HBA audience to feel that it was their special visit.

Using a PR, press and social media strategy for the roadshow, we created a buzz ensuring maximum interest and media coverage. This brought the added benefit of creating broader brand awareness of the Sundial Group, with an impact that lasted beyond the duration on the actual roadshow.

The roadshow's design

As a family business with many years of experience and unique philosophy and values we felt we had a remarkable story to tell, and Sundial's senior management team was there, on the roadshow, to tell it: Tim Chudley, our Group Managing Director, took on the role of bus driver and story-teller; Mia Butler, our Agency Sales Manager, acted as the tour manager; and Jerry Toth, our Group Executive Head Chef, cooked al-fresco at each destination. The fact that members of our senior management team were present on the roadshow was a critical factor in establishing the personal rapport and trust that achieving our objectives required.

The vehicle used for the roadshow was a double-decker bus that we called the 'Chudbus'. The story of the original Chudbus is told on a Gaumont newsreel, now posted on YouTube (http://www.youtube.com/watch?v=TfRpegkyuGw). In the late 1950s, Tim Chudley's parents took him and his five siblings on a holiday tour of America in a bus which they purchased and fitted up especially for that family holiday.

Although the original Chudbus story predated the formation of the Sundial Group, we felt that it provided a fascinating means of adding personality to our company. When the London Routemaster fleet of double-decker buses was decommissioned in 2005, we had purchased one of them and used it as an exhibition vehicle and occasional meeting space. Making creative use of a bus that was an authentic and documented link to the Chudley family and the Sundial Group provided us with a unique and memorable setting in which to talk about the experience, philosophy and values that underpin our venue products and services. And having the story told by Tim Chudley who featured as a young child in the newsreel added extra authenticity and excitement.

The ever-popular 1963 movie, 'Summer Holiday', in which the singer Cliff Richard and a group of friends spend a holiday driving a double-decker bus around Europe, supplied the roadshow's title, Summer Holiday Tour.

The Chudbus, completely refurbished to showcase state-of-the-art conference furnishings and technology exactly as offered in our venues, vividly demonstrated to our HBA guests the quality of the meetings environment in Sundial Group venues. Moreover, the smells and taste of the cookery demonstration and the fresh hot food provided for our guests stimulated their senses and provided a taste of the quality of our catering. In this way, the creativity and quality of the roadshow event directly demonstrated what the HBAs' clients can expect from our venues and established creativity as a point of difference for our brand.

Photo: The Chudbus Roadshow, courtesy Sundial

Execution of the roadshow

Posters and a social media campaign were used to stimulate excitement and HBAs' engagement with the roadshow, prior to each visit to their premises.

The Chudbus Summer Holiday Tour is Coming to YOU!

This tour is set to be Sundial's best yet with promises of a 'Summer Holiday' soundtrack, non-alcoholic cocktails, and a Spanish Paella being cooked fresh on the day!

Not to mention, the chance to **WIN A HOLIDAY TO SPAIN!**

Our Sundial Venues Summer Holiday Tour aims to bring a bit of Sundial to you!

Where: Your carpark!

When: Wednesday 29th June

From 1230 – 2pm

All aboard – hop on The Chudbus!!
You will be made very welcome
We look forward to seeing you there!

Mia

Mia Butler, Agency Sales Manager | mia.butler@sundialgroup.com | www.sundialvenues.com | 07974 822757

Each visit began by us parking the Chudbus in a reserved space outside the HBAs' office front door. Jerry cooked garlic, onions and white wine stock, as the initial step in the preparation of a giant paella. Half an hour of delicious smells wafting through their offices ensured that no HBA wanted to miss the opportunity to visit our bus!

In groups of from 6 to 12, the venue bookers broke for lunch, and headed for the Chudbus. After collecting their paella, the groups assembled on the lower deck of the bus, seated in our high-quality conference chairs. The 1959 Gaumont newsreel was

4

shown on the on-board plasma screen, and Tim talked about the development of Sundial Group and the characteristics that make it an award-winning benchmark for residential venues. This was followed by an engaging presentation of our properties given by Mia, during which she was able to talk about numerous bespoke events we have hosted, demonstrating our flexibility and customer focus.

Agents enjoying paella as guests on the Chudbus road show

The informal conversations that followed these presentations enabled Tim, Mia and Jerry to find out more about the HBAs' clients and identify opportunities for business development. They also established personal relationships between the Sundial Group management and the HBAs, making it easy for us to maintain links to the venue bookers after the visit. Engagement with the bookers was also extended through the use of a fun caption competition. This involved handing out a holiday prize competition entry form to everyone who came on board the bus during the road show, and inviting them to create a caption. The prize for the best entry was – inevitably – a summer holiday. This was an effective way of capturing their contact details and enabled us to follow up after the visit with news of progress throughout the summer – keeping us front of mind for an extended period.

The upper deck of the bus was furnished with our marketing materials and sticks of Sundial rock which our guests took happily back to their desks after the presentation.

Agents attending a presentation on the upper deck of the Chudbus

The evaluation and review process

The following methods were used to evaluate the success of our roadshow:

■ Evaluation metrics were produced from Sundial's CRM and bookings system, by comparing numbers of enquiries and the value of HBA-derived revenue before, during and after the roadshow.

■ On-the-day enquiries were monitored and tracked in order to measure the immediate impact of each visit of the roadshow.

■ The extent to which the roadshow generated additional exposure for our venues was calculated by comparing the number of HBA office presentations that we normally achieve in that period of time with the number of agencies allowing us in for the first time as a result of our Summer Holiday Tour.

■ We monitored Twitter and other social media as well as all of the industry-specific media to detect the number of mentions of #Chudbus and to monitor the growth of new 'followers' for @sundialtim the driver. The number of contacts that we received from the media for editorial or news contributions and comment were also tracked.

Results:

- Our roadshow generated an additional £374,000 of HBA revenue, an increase of 60% for the Sundial Group. The £10k budget therefore had an ROI of 37:1.

- The value of on-the-day enquiries alone exceeded £55,000.

- The proportion of agency business lost between RFP and confirmation was reduced by 35% between - 350% of our objective.

- We gained access to the bookers at a number of significant agencies that were high on our target list. In all, we presented to 290 individual bookers.

- Agency Select Partnerships were agreed with 3 of the largest UK-based international agencies.

- The tour was tweeted and re-tweeted more than 300 times, broadcasting messages such as from Find Me A Conference, 'A special #ff @mia_butler @sundialtim @jochudley lovely people, lovely venues and lovely paella! Thanks for a great showcase!' and email, 'Thank you for such a great effort with the team lunch last week! The feedback has been brilliant, please do pass our thanks to everyone involved with the Chudbus!'. A Director of Procurement

- @sundialtim increased its number of followers by 250%, and trade editorial and news coverage was secured on at least 8 occasions.

- Tim's Blog - http://sundialtim.blogspot.co.uk/2011/05/chudbus-on-tour.html received several hundred page-views.

- Four agencies ask to rebook visits for the following year's Chudbus tour even before it was announced.

The Chudbus tour to Hotel Booking Agents has now become an eagerly anticipated annual event and has been expanded to include visits to direct corporate client offices.

Lessons

Venues should not be afraid of trying an innovative approach to promoting themselves in the market. As long as they stay true to their product and brand, clients and prospects will always value an original approach to getting their message across. This is what Sundial aimed to deliver with the Chudbus Summer Holiday roadshow, and we found that it was extremely effective in reaching our target customers.

Also, businesses often have interesting stories behind them. With the Chudbus, we shaped one of our stories so that it became relevant as a marketing initiative. Businesses which look to their past may discover something new and unique to share with their customers. Effective CRM is about interaction on a personal level, so businesses that tell a good story, can infuse their brands' values with personality. At Sundial, customers identify with us differently than with our competitors. The Chudbus is one example of how we have remained personal even though we are now a multi-site operator providing meeting facilities across the UK.

The role of convention and visitor bureaus

Convention and visitor bureaus (CVBs) are important intermediaries that play a key role in promoting destinations and attracting meetings and other events to the countries and cities they represent. As destination marketing organisations, CVBs are important information brokers and disseminators in the meetings and events sector. The vast majority of CVBs operate at the city level, but there are also examples of national CVBs, that are responsible for promoting their entire country as a destination for business events.

In their efforts to solicit meetings business for their destinations, the principal role of most CVBs is to brand and market their destination to those who are responsible for selecting destinations for their meetings and events. But many also provide a variety of useful services to meeting planners. Polivka (1996) detailed the various tasks that CVBs perform for meeting planners. For example, they can organise familiarisation trips for meeting planners, to stimulate their interest in the destination. They can suggest reliable and appropriate service providers in their destination, from DMCs and caterers to accommodation and venues. They can also circulate information to venues in the form of requests for proposals (RFPs) that they receive directly from organisations interested in holding an event in their destination.

Other CVB activities pertaining to the servicing of conferences include:

☐   'attendance building' – the promotion of the event with the aim of boosting attendance numbers

☐   assistance with finding accommodation for conference delegates

☐   on-site registration and information.

☐   Some CVBs can also offer subvention – financial support – to associations bringing their conferences to the destination.

According to Vallee (2008, p.162-163), a CVB most commonly achieves its goals by working to:

☐   Solicit, qualify, and confirm groups to hold meetings, conventions, and trade shows in the area it represents;

☐   Assist meeting groups that have confirmed through attendance building and convention servicing;

☐   Manage the destination brand through awareness building and customer relationship management;

☐   Market to leisure travel trade and individual travellers through targeted promotional and sales activities;

☐   Facilitate relationships between meeting manager and travel trade buyers and sellers, with sellers generally composed of local businesses offering products and services;

☐   Service visitors, including convention delegates, in the destination to encourage them to stay longer and see more of the area.

From the meeting planners' perspective, a CVB is a 'one-stop-shop'. They often prefer to use services provided by CVBs instead of other institutions because CVBs' services can satisfy their needs for unbiased information on venues and other suppliers. CVB websites usually serve as the destination's official presence on the Internet. These websites provide extensive information about the services of the CVBs as well as useful information on meetings facilities and services, hotel accommodation, etc.

Spin With Berlin – The Berlin UK Roadshow 2013

How a convention bureau worked with venues on a novel way of reaching out to agencies

Marco Oelschlegel, Senior Marketing Manager Conventions, Berlin Convention Office

Berlin as a meetings destination

The German capital's success as a meetings destination is in no doubt. For many years, Berlin has appeared in the top 5 of the most successful cities for international association meetings as complied by ICCA. The appeal of Berlin for the UK tourist market is in clear. According to the 2013 statistics published by visitBerlin, the destination marketing organisation with responsibility for promoting the city world-wide, the UK is Berlin's most important source market for visitors from abroad, with over 10% of the total share of overnights. The city is also one of the most attractive cities for corporate meetings of UK-based companies. Berlin's strength of popularity with UK agencies may be seen in the example given in Figure 4.1, where venues in the city were nominated twice in response to a theoretical brief for a product launch given to four agencies. And the winning pitch, as selected by the 'client', was for one of the Berlin-based events.

The Berlin Convention Office

The visitBerlin Berlin Convention Office (BCO) has been the official representative of Berlin as a meeting destination since 1 July 2001. Since that date, the BCO has won a number of prestigious prizes for their work, some of the most recent examples of which are:

■ In 2010, the German capital was presented with the World Travel Award 2010 by the leading business travel magazine 'Business Destinations'. Berlin won in the category 'Best Destination for M.I.C.E, Western Europe'.

■ In 2011, at the Business Destinations Awards, the Berlin Convention Office of visit-Berlin came out on top in two categories. It received prizes in the categories 'Best Value for Money, Europe' and 'Best Hotel Landscape, Europe'.

The BCO is a department of visitBerlin, a public-private partnership with support from the local government (the city of Berlin). In its role of promoting Berlin as a meetings and events destination, the BCO cooperates with a number of strategic partners in the city including the visitBerlin Partnerhotels and the visitBerlin Preferred Agencies associations, as well as the Senate of Berlin (government) . It is a member of several international alliances and associations such as BestCities Global Alliance, ICCA, GCB, ECM, Eventia, MPI and SITE.

Marketing Berlin in the UK

One of the tools employed by the BCO is the organising of an annual event in the UK, which has the objective of bringing together face-to-face representatives from BCO's strategic partners with UK buyers. The first of these events - Berlin Meets London - was held in 2008 at the Imagination Gallery in London, and subsequent events were held at The Gallery Soho, altitude 360°, The Hospital Club and the London Film Museum

In 2013, the BCO experimented with a new concept: a cycling trip through England, stopping along the way to meet with key agency buyers at their own places of work.

Product in search of a setting that matches its cutting-edge style

The brief is for a two-day launch to 200 key Europe-based clients and retailers. The location and venue should mirror the client's 'fresh, different, cutting edge' marketing, with conference space for 200 and a breakout for 50

Alan Wight managing director, Cascade Productions

1

Tracy Sorgiovanni account director, RPM

2

Denise Warner project director, Logistik

3

Alex Beckett director, DV8 Global Events

4

We would suggest linking the theme to the programme – having elements of 'fresh', 'different' and 'cutting edge' throughout – making the whole experience the message. We'd choose a traditional venue like **L'Impérial Palace Annecy**, France, alongside the cleanest lake in Europe, and add contrasting 'fresh', modern dressing. 'Different' would be in every detail: invitations, travel, dressing on the lakeside terrace; everything. 'Cutting edge' would be in the delivery of the message, the tools to communicate the key features and benefits, digital projection, RFID, and mobile app. The location allows for surprises in the itinerary and even the menus should surprise with fresh ingredients and different flavours. Every aspect of the event should make the experience the message: location, venue, tech, dressing, itinerary, meeting tools and programme all combining to create an effective event.

I would propose to hold the product launch at the **Humboldt-Box** in Berlin. The German capital has a reputation as arty and edgy but is now also an up-and-coming destination for high-tech start-ups, with Google recently opening a new office there. It is also well connected for ease of travel across Europe.

Located in the heart of Berlin, on Museum Island, the Humboldt-Box is an architectural work of art across five floors that would epitomise the 'fresh, different and cutting-edge' nature of the product. The launch event would take place in the Sky-lounge on the fourth floor, with panoramic windows affording spectacular views for up to 220 seated delegates. The fifth floor is available as a smaller breakout space. The **Radisson Blu Hotel** is within a short walk of the venue and would comfortably accommodate all 200 guests for the overnight stay.

Fresh, different and cutting edge meant my initial thought was a city, with bright lights, buzzing atmosphere and cutting-edge architecture. But to bring in the fresh element, surely that has to include a sea breeze and a breathtaking view.

So the destination I would choose is **Hvar Island, Croatia**. It is glamorous, chic, unspoilt, and full of beautiful people, which is perfect for a product launch. It's an island, so you get an exclusive feel and it's far from run of the mill. Great access for Europeans, with the option to do private boat transfers from the airport adding that extra 'wow', which clients always look for at events that include customers.

I would suggest staying at **Amfora Grand Beach Resort**. It has plenty of meeting space and would be able to cope with the 200 plus 50 for breakout. People flying in would arrive at Split Airport and flight access is extremely good with regular scheduled flights.

Driving attendance from a mixed client and retailer audience is key – Berlin offers good rail and air links from most major European hubs.

With 304 bedrooms on the banks of the river Spree, the **Nhow Berlin** is a forward-thinking concept, combining urban lifestyle, fashion and cutting-edge technology. The hotel's Music Hall conference room will house the main product launch for 200 guests, while the Gallery provides an urban backdrop for the product experience for 50 delegates.

Originally an electrical sub-station, the **Ewerk** building has played host to memorable moments in Berlin's cultural history. With a drinks reception on the rooftop terrace, guests will enjoy panoramic views of the city, followed by dinner served in the adjacent lounge.

Digital communications would support the event, using web-based interaction and registration pre-event, and app-based content during the launch.

THE CLIENT VERDICT **Janel Snider, Innocent Drinks**

I would choose Agency 4. Its approach was clear, highlighting the importance of accessibility, while still offering a unique venue. They met the brief and provided other add-ons. I liked the idea of digital communications supporting the event. It is both sustainable and current, with

app-based content being really interesting. However, I would be curious how the agency would ensure delegates engage.

Agency 1 did a great job tying the theme into the pitch and I loved the principle that the venue should never be more memorable than the product. However, it was too conceptual.

Agency 2's pitch was similar to Agency 4's but lacked the

Forward-thinking Nhow Berlin

enthusiasm and attention to detail. They met the brief, but did not think beyond to provide alternative ideas.

I liked Agency 3's idea of an exclusive resort, but felt that the logistics of getting all the guests there would be too complicated.

Environment project co-ordinator Janel Snider judged the pitches without knowing wh submitted them.

CITMAGAZINE.C

Figure 4.1: The Agency Challenge results

The initiative was formally launched at the M&IT Industry Awards event held in London in March 2013 and organised by CAT publications. At that occasion, the BCO's director of conventions, Heike Mahmoud said: "We ask all UK meeting planners to give us a break. Literally! Tell us where to meet you and we will stop by ... Take a moment to hear what we want to achieve for Berlin, the businesses supporting us and the charities we are supporting. We chose cycling, the greenest form of transport, to bolster the notion that Berlin is a green, sustainable and active city and to show planners: This is the perfect destination for meetings, conventions and incentives!"

The goal was for the participants in the roadshow to cycle approximately 120km a day, with the agency meeting planners encountered on the tour being encouraged to take their own bikes and join in the 'Spin with Berlin' event for a while.

The roadshow

From 10 - 13 June 2013, representatives from the BCO and their hotel and venue partners cycled through England to promote their city and their venues to 13 UK-based agencies. The Spin with Berlin tour began in Leeds and finished in London, after passing through cities such as Derby and Milton Keynes, where stops were made at leading UK meetings and events agencies, with three main objectives:

- to network

- to present Berlin´s qualities as a convention and incentive destination

- to raise money for two charity projects: Meeting Industry Meeting Needs in the UK; and a Berlin based charity, Hand-in-Hand.

The BCO's partners who took part in this roadshow were a combination of venues, hotels and other suppliers of services and facilities to the meetings industry:

Andel's Hotel Berlin	Ellington Hotel Berlin
Estrel Berlin	Grand Hyatt Berlin
Hollywood Media Hotel	Hotel Palace Berlin
Regent Hotel Berlin	Scandic Potsdamer Platz
Pullman Berlin Schweizerhof	AXICA (venue)
BESL (venue & agency)	Conference & Touring (agency)
Lufthansa (airline)	visitBerlin Berlin Convention Office

BCO's media partner for this event was CAT publications. They covered the roadshow from beginning to end and supported the charity initiative associated with it. The

PR and Social Media campaigns for Spin with Berlin began three months before the actual event.

In preparation for the cycling trip, the participants got into training many months before the roadshow began. The plan was to put all participants into pairs sharing one bicycle, so that everyone had a 'bike buddy'. Through this system, the participants took turns cycling, while their bike-buddy rested by travelling on the group's vehicle.

On 10 June 2013, the participants flew from Berlin to Birmingham, where they were met by the group's coach, painted red and clearly branded with an image of Berlin's skyline and the slogan: 'Berlin: the place to be for conventions'.

At every stop made at agencies' offices, the roadshow participants were warmly received and great interest was expressed in the Berlin venues and hotels represented. The agencies appreciated this novel way of meeting Berlin suppliers of meetings facilities, and at each stage of the journey their reactions to being visited by the Berlin cyclists was overwhelmingly positive. As an example, following a visit to one agency, one of their meeting planners tweeted: "Unique, alternative way to meet! Great to get a better understanding of the destination and what it offers!" And at the group's stop in Leeds, the agency's whole team turned out to welcome the cyclists on the street.

At one stop on the roadshow, instead of the six meeting planners that were expected to turn out to meet the cyclists, forty showed up. Why? The answer is probably best provided by the comment of one meeting planner: "It is a great way of getting out of the boardroom and death by PowerPoint!"

Evaluating the success of Spin with Berlin

There is no doubt that in terms of its coverage on the social media, this event surpassed the expectations of all participants. This was the first of the BCO's annual events in the UK for which a blog was created, enabling the public to follow the trip's progress throughout the event, from the preparation stage to the conclusion. This extended the reach of the publicity around the event and enabled much more interaction with different audiences.

Links to the blog were retweeted 187 times. It had 291 mentions and earned @Berlinmeetings 109 new followers.

11 of the visited agencies are on Twitter, and the vast majority of them interacted with @Berlinmeetings and posted Tweets about #spinBerlin. Several representatives of the agencies also used their private Twitter accounts to tweet about "Spin with Berlin".

In all, the representatives of Berlin's meeting industry saw 13 top UK agencies during their cycling tour, and at each one they saw more meeting planners than they had expected to: over one hundred in total, which was more than they had ever been able to see at previous events they had organised in London. These meeting planners were genuine decision-makers and influencers, and gaining access to them in this way was extremely effective in spreading the word about Berlin's assets as a destination for meetings.

The initiative of 'Spin for Berlin' earned the organisers a nomination for the MIMA Awards in the category "Best Live Marketing Award". And, last but not least, £3261.70 was raised for the two charities, from the Berlin partners and the agencies they visited.

How venues can work effectively with CVBs

Venues that are fortunate enough to be located in cities served by a CVB need to understand how to work most effectively with them. Collaborative efforts between venues and their CVBs can bring those venues a number of important advantages – but only if they take the time to work fully in partnership with their CVB.

Most CVBs have a membership structure. In return for paying an annual fee, a venue can become a member of their local CVB, which gives it some influence in its activities and focus. But many venues make the mistake of simply paying their fees and sitting back waiting for results. The more enlightened venues understand that it is essential to be an active member and to work hard at building a constructive relationship, so that they can work in partnership with their CVB to offer clients unique and attractive solutions.

■ CVB services

What services can a CVB offer local venues?

☐ Many CVBs compile and publish – either on their website or (increasingly rarely) in print directories – listings of their members for the attention of meetings planners looking for somewhere to hold their event.

☐ The CVB may have an enquiry service, through which they receive requests for proposals (RFPs) from organisations seeking a venue in their destination. Most CVBs with membership structures will give priority to those venues that are fully paid-up members and that meet the enquirer's criteria, by sending them these RFPs first. However, venue managers need to constantly take steps to ensure that when the staff of their local CVB receive an RFP, they remember to send it to their venue. In order to act as an effective source of potential bookings, CVB staff need to have a clear and up-to-date understanding of each venue's characteristics, capacities, and relevant developments such as refurbishments and extensions. It is the venue manager's responsibility to keep the CVB updated on such developments, by, for example, regularly inviting CVB staff into the venue for a show-around or a networking event.

☐ CVBs can provide venues in their destination with a cost-effective way of exhibiting at meetings industry trade shows, when they offer them the opportunity of sharing the CVB's stand. (See Chapter 6). But even when (usually for financial reasons) venues are not able to send a member of their staff to an exhibition, they can still be promoted by the CVB staff who do attend – if those staff have adequate and up-to-date knowledge of the venue, as well as the necessary promotional material.

☐ Many larger CVBs have sales representatives permanently based in countries around the world that are key sources of demand, and a major aspect of their role is to help promote their city's venues to potential buyers

☐ Some CVBs run regular sales-missions or sales-trips to countries that represent actual or potential sources of demand for business events in their destinations. For example, many European CVBs organise sales missions to American cities to meet US-based international association managers in their own offices. The CVBs usually take along a few selected partners with them to see prospects and make sales presentations to them. Those venues normally pay an extra fee for this opportunity, but the advantage is that it is the CVB that makes the appointments with potential buyers.

☐ There are other types of events that CVBs may organise in order to bring their members face-to-face with potential buyers. These include appointment-based workshops, usually in the form of table-top meetings; or simple networking events, bringing together buyers and suppliers in a more informal social setting.

☐ Most CVBs issue regular newsletters, and other publications that they send out to their mailing lists of potential clients and other stakeholders. These provide venues with the opportunity to widely disseminate information on new developments in their facility or on events that they have successfully secured or hosted.

☐ Ambassador programmes are growing in popularity as CVB-led initiatives that harness the power of members of the local scientific, academic or business community to bring conferences to the destination in which they are based. CVBs are usually the catalyst for the creating and managing of Ambassador Programmes. They recruit academics and researchers from local universities, for example, giving preference to those who are members of national and international associations. The CVB then takes steps to motivate these local 'ambassadors' to lobby for their associations to bring their conferences to their city. Most Ambassador

4

Programmes are long-term investments, in the sense that they rarely produce instant results, but nevertheless, venues can and should get involved by, for example, attending the networking and educational events organised by their CVB, for ambassadors. It may even be possible for a venue to approach its CVB with the idea of creating an Ambassador Programme where none already exists.

Girona Ambassadors

Palau de Congressos de Girona, photo by Aniol Resclosa

In 2010, the Girona Conference Centre (Palau de Congressos de Girona) (www.gironacongressos.org) in cooperation with the Costa Brava Girona Convention Bureau (www.gironacb.com) began a programme of targeting medical professionals in their city, with the aim of motivating them to use their connections in the fields of medicine in order to win conferences for Girona.

For the medical professionals, the Conference Centre and Convention Bureau run an annual training session at Girona's Josep Trueta Hospital, using the hospital's theatre as an auditorium for the event. During the training session, representatives from the conference centre and convention bureau explain to the doctors how conference planners choose destinations for their events and how the medical professionals can use their influence as members of national and international associations and research groups, in order to bring medical conferences to Girona. A key intermediary is the person in charge of communication for the Josep Trueta Hospital, who informs the medical staff about these training sessions and motivates them to participate.

During these sessions, the conference centre and convention bureau representatives explain the various ways in which they can provide logistical assistance and support to any doctor who agrees to work with them in bidding to bring a conference to Girona. They also describe the city's attractions as a conference destination, as well as the facilities and services offered by the Girona Conference Centre.

But the principal objective of these training sessions is to reassure the medical professionals that they would be fully supported in any attempt they make to win a conference for their city. As a result of these sessions, a number of medical conferences are already in the pipeline for Girona. Following this success, the conference centre and convention bureau decided to target professors at the city's University, with the same objective of encouraging them to bring conferences to their city.

4

☐   Perhaps one of the most beneficial activities of CVBs is their responsibility for bidding for national and international association conferences. Such organisations often choose the destinations for their events by inviting cities to bid in order to host it – a form of competitive tendering process. Central to the whole process is the Bid Document, which is generally compiled by the CVB, and which includes a great deal of technical information that will help the association to evaluate the city's suitability as a destination for their conference: hotel capacity, flight times, flight frequencies, and so on. The CVB also puts into the document details of one or more local venues that would be able to host the conference in question, including the venues' capacities and rates. Again, it is essential that venues keep their local CVBs completely up-to-date with changes and developments, so that the CVB is able to judge accurately which venues should be included in the Bid Document.

It would not be cost-effective, in terms of the use of any CVB's resources, for it to bid for each and every conference in search of a destination. That is why professionally managed CVBs tend to have a strategy to bid for those conferences that have the best 'fit' with the destination. It is vital for venues in the destination to align themselves with this strategy by ensuring that they offer the range and standard of facilities and services required to host the type or types of conferences for which their CVB generally bids.

Clearly, CVBs can offer local venues a wide range of benefits by acting as a disseminator of information about those venues as well as channelling potential business in their direction. But it is certainly worth repeating what was stated earlier – that simply paying a membership fee to their local CVB does not guarantee that a venue will be automatically able to reap the full range of benefits from the services listed above. A partnership approach, with the venue and its CVB working closely together, is key to maximising the advantages of being located in a city served by a CVB. Some larger venues have gone as far as to designate a member of staff with specific responsibility for liaising with the CVB, to ensure that the venue benefits fully from the services that the CVB provides.

In addition to venues communicating regularly with their CVB, the CVB itself must also keep their members informed of developments in the destination that may affect its appeal as a place for the hosting of events: new air connections, entertainment options, new dining opportunities for offsite gala dinners, for example. When negotiating with out-of-town prospects who have not already chosen the destination for their forthcoming event, this kind of information can be crucial to a successful outcome for the venue.

Cooperation between venues and CVBs is most effective when there is an efficient and regular two-way communication between them both.

The World Justice Forum in The Hague

Winning a major conference as a result of close collaboration between a venue and its CVB

The Venue: The World Forum

The World Forum (www.worldforum.nl) is a congress centre in the Dutch city of The Hague, which is known as the city of peace and justice. The venue is owned by The Hague's municipality and is managed by the French company, GL events. GL events manages thirty-five convention centres worldwide, from Barcelona to Shanghai, and also has many years of experience in the organising of events. The company was founded over 30 years ago and now has a presence on all five continents and more than 3500 employees.

Conferences such as those of the International Criminal Court (ICC) and the OPCW (Organisation for the Prohibition of Chemical Weapons), which have been held in this venue, represent dialogues at the highest levels of international relations and law. And in 2009, the World Forum successfully hosted the largest peace conference to be held in the Netherlands since the Second World War: the United Nations summit on Afghanistan, attended by 73 delegations from all over the world.

Along with such high profile conferences, the World Forum also hosts corporate events, association conferences, receptions and exhibitions. The venue has 15,000 m² of rooms, of which 10,000 m² may be used as exhibition space. Its 27 rooms vary in capacity from a boardroom for 10 people to an auditorium with a capacity of 2,161 delegates. The auditorium is surrounded by 26 break-out rooms.

The destination marketing organisation: The Hague Convention Bureau

The Hague Convention Bureau (www.thehaguecongress.com) is a not-for-profit organization with responsibility for promoting the city of The Hague as a business events destination. It is a department of The Hague Marketing (Den Haag Marketing), the umbrella marketing and promotion organisation for The Hague and its two beach resorts, Scheveningen and Kijkduin. The Hague Convention Bureau is funded through two sources: the Municipality of The Hague and annual fees paid by its members. It has a staff of three. In addition to its destination marketing role, The Hague Convention Bureau offers a number of valuable services for suppliers in the city and for meeting planners:

■   Tailor-made advice on relevant facilities, services and selected suppliers.

- Organising networking meetings between potential organisers and suppliers.

- Organising site visits and familiarisation trips.

- Setting up and assisting in bid procedures.

- Providing advice on social programmes, incentives and partner programmes.

- Distributing promotional materials.

The client: The World Justice Project. The event: The World Justice Forum, 8-11 July 2013

The World Justice Project is an independent, non-profit organization that develops communities of opportunity and equity by advancing the rule of law worldwide. The organisation engages leaders in countries across the globe in order to advance the rule of law. Its principal aim is to encourage government reforms, through developing practical on-the-ground programmes that increase understanding of how the rule of law is important to people and the communities where they live. The World Justice Forum (WJF) is an annual global gathering organised by the WJP, designed to improve the state of the world by engaging leaders from business, government, civil society, academia, and other domains to develop practical, multidisciplinary programmes to strengthen the rule of law. The event provides a platform for leaders and change agents from all disciplines to explore and debate crucial rule-of-law issues, with a focus on shared learning and collaboration. During the three days of the Forum, participants from more than 100 countries engage in formal plenary and active breakout sessions, where they learn about innovative rule-of-law programmes. They interact with researchers and scholars during workshop hours, and network with other leaders from different disciplines. The Forum also provides the opportunity for discussion and debate about the findings of the World Justice Project Role of Law Index, an innovative assessment tool that measures how well countries adhere to the rule of law in practice.

http://worldjusticeproject.org/world-justice-forum-iv/home

Winning the World Justice Forum for The Hague

In February 2012, the first contact between the World Justice Project and the World Forum took place, following political discussions between the Municipality of The Hague and the Ministry of Safety and Justice.

After receiving a formal Request for Proposal from the WJP, The Hague Convention Bureau then contacted the Municipality to seek their views on whether or not it would be worthwhile attempting to bring the World Justice Forum to their city. Until this point, the Hague Convention Bureau had not been involved in discussions between their Municipality and the WJP. When the Municipality told them that they really wanted to have the WJF in The Hague, The Hague Convention Bureau and the World Forum began the process of competing to win that event.

In March 2012, The Hague Convention Bureau and the World Forum met to discuss the venue's availability and how the WJF could be organised in the venue and throughout the city as a whole. They agreed that the best strategy would be for both organisations to work together on the bid, together with local hotels, and with the support of the Municipality and the Ministry of Safety and Justice. As part of their work on preparing a response to the Request for Proposal, they requested that local hotels hold rooms for the proposed dates of the WJF.

By May 2012, it became clear that there was strong competition for this event from two other potential destinations: Barcelona and Istanbul.

In June 2012, a successful meeting took place between the WJP on the one hand and The Hague Convention Bureau and the Municipality on the other hand, when the President of the WJP visited the Netherlands. At that meeting, the bid from The Hague was presented.

In July 2012, it was announced that the World Justice Project had chosen The Hague as the destination for its 2013 World Justice Forum.

The World Justice Project at the World Forum. Source: worldjusticeproject.org/

The World Justice Project, plenary session. Source: worldjusticeproject.org/

Presenting findings from the WJP Rule of Law Index. Source: worldjusticeproject.org/

Nancy Ward, Chief Engagement Officer of the World Justice Project

Cooperation with The Hague Convention Bureau

The World Justice Project's experience with The Hague Convention Bureau began during talks with the Municipality of The Hague, and the actions of the HCB were critically instrumental in our decision to bring the World Justice Forum to that city. Bart Klaver, the HCB's Account Manager: Associations, was available for multiple phone conversations as we were considering the city as our venue, and he had the authority to help broker financial deals with various entities in The Hague that made the budget work for us from the very beginning. David Bodor, the HCB's Strategic Marketing Officer, made all of the arrangements for my initial site visit to the city in July 2012 after we had made the decision to bring the WJF to The Hague, including complimentary hotel reservations and meetings with The Hague Marketing. My site visit included meetings with transportation and tourism suppliers; tours of restaurants for special events; and a bike tour of the city with a guide. Throughout the following months, when I had many questions that needed answers, David's responsiveness and high quality guidance were invaluable to the success of our conference and also to my peace of mind. Another considerable benefit to us was the HCB's free-access photograph library, which was a real asset to the attractiveness and effectiveness of our online marketing and print materials for the conference. The HCB also provided direct assistance with the arrangement of signage around the city advertising the WJF, and brokered access to public transport passes and refunds for the portions we did not use. They also provided a dedicated on-site staff member to offer tourism services, recommendations and materials during the Forum. This was a big difference from past events and really made our participants feel welcome in the city. The HCB even offered access to child care providers – that is just one more example of how their staff consistently went above and beyond duty. Although almost everything was set in place by the time the Forum began, I had the security of knowing that I had the full resources of the city supporting us, should we need anything at any point. This is a considerable comfort for a small organisation like ours, when hosting a global conference.

Cooperation with the World Forum

The WJP would not have held this meeting in The Hague without absolute confidence in the management of the World Forum. The information that they made available to us from the very start of our evaluation and planning process was complete and easy to navigate. The World Forum management worked with the HCB to provide us with a competitive pricing structure that made it possible for us to commit to the venue, even with our limited resources. During my site visit, I was introduced to the managers of every department within the World Forum who would be working with us to provide services on site. Those meetings allowed me to understand not only what was available but also to appreciate the professionalism of the staff who would be creating and supporting our experience at the conference centre. Daphne Vreeburg, Project Manager at the World Forum, gave me a good baseline plan early in the process, and even recalibrated her reporting to a view that I could more easily understand. The format and clarity of the BEO [Banquet Event Order: a document that outlines all of the details of the event and serves as a guideline for the venue to execute and communicate logistics to all necessary departments] from the venue worked well for me throughout the planning process and made the review of the final portfolio very quick and easy. Daphne was extremely patient for the months I delayed review of this service plan, and was highly responsive and creative in solutions when I finally got around to finalising the details. Though we had a limited budget to create a world-class experience, she nevertheless helped us craft the best possible physical platform we could. The nature of our agenda – with multiple small breakout groups – stretched the capacity of the venue, but Daphne figured out how to move sessions around and deliver what we needed even though it meant using the building in different ways from usual. She was a vital bridge to all of the individual staff members and suppliers, helping us solve problems and ensuring that the event itself ran smoothly. Every member of staff that I worked with was friendly, kind, efficient, and effective. This venue itself is not only an attractive facility but an incredibly well-managed enterprise that easily surpasses the quality of any other venue I've worked in over the past 20 years of international meetings.

To summarise, I would say that the most outstanding benefits we experienced through working with the HCB and the World Forum were the high levels of service and responsiveness (professionalism), the relationships they were able to broker (trust), and the discounts they could arrange (competitive/comparative costs).

Sources

Hatch, S. (2013) 'Unraveling the Mysteries of Event Planner Pricing' *MeetingsNet*, February 12

McInnes, W. (1964) 'A Conceptual Approach to Marketing', in R. Cox, W. Alderson, and S. Shapiro (eds) *Theory in Marketing*, pp. 51–67. Homewood, IL: Richard D. Irwin.

Polivka, E. G. (Ed.). (1996). *Professional meeting management* (3rd ed.). Birmingham, AL: Professional Convention Management Association.

Shaw, E. H. (2013) 'The Quest for a General Theory of the Marketing System', in *Proceedings of Conference on Historical Analysis and Research in Marketing (CHARM)*, Vol. 16

Vallee P. (2008), Convention and Visitors Bureaus: Partnering with Meeting Managers for Success, in Ramsborg G. C., Miller B., Breiter D., Reed B. J., and Rushing A. (ed.), *Comprehensive Strategies for Meetings, Conventions and Events Professional Meeting Management*, Professional Convention Management Association, pp 161-178, 5th edition, Kendall/Hunt Publishing Company

Online sources of further information

International Congress and Convention Association (ICCA): Working with Convention Bureaux.
www.iccaworld.com/cdps/cditem.cfm?nid=4086

Hotel Booking Agents Association: Money for Nothing. Get your cheques for free? Payment models in the meetings market.
www.hbaa.org.uk/document-store

4

5 Site Inspections

Types of site inspection

In Chapter 3, the practice of key account management was discussed. In Chapter 6, the use of face-to-face selling techniques at exhibitions will be explored. A powerful element of – or follow-on from – these two techniques is to invite prospects into the venue so that they can see it for themselves, at first hand.

In this sense, site inspections are the ultimate form of experiential marketing for venues. Experiential marketing may be defined as a form of advertising that focuses primarily on helping consumers experience a brand. As such, it may be distinguished from traditional advertising (radio, print, television), which verbally and visually communicates the product benefits. Experiential marketing, by way of contrast, tries to immerse consumers within the product by engaging as many other human senses as possible.

Also known as show-rounds, site inspections involve providing a pre-arranged tour of the venue for two principal sources of business: prospects and agencies. A third category of visitors to the venue, for the purposes of a site inspection, is the press – journalists carrying out research for an article they are writing for a trade magazine aimed at those working in the meetings industry.

Such tours can be either individual or in groups. Site inspections may be organised independently by the venue, or they may form part of a broader familiarisation trip or press trip, usually organised by a convention bureau.

In larger venues, the site inspection may be conducted by a member of the sales team. In venues that are too small to have a sales team, any manager may find themselves having responsibility for showing their venue to prospects or agencies.

There are two possible stages in the sales cycle when a site inspection may occur:

☐　The first is at the very beginning of the sales cycle, when a prospect or agency has no immediate need for a venue for a particular event, but has been persuaded to visit the venue to get an overview of the facilities and experience them for themselves, so that they may consider it for their future meetings and events. This type of site inspection is occasionally called a venue tour, but venue managers who simply show the visitor around the venue are not making the most of the opportunity that such inspections can offer. The prospect may not have an immediate need for a venue, but their visit to the venue offers a useful opportunity for the venue manager to spend time with them, before, during or after the tour, discussing their future requirements and establishing to what extent there is a synergy between those requirements and the venue's facilities and services. In this situation, the site visit may be used as an extension of the lead qualifying process that was described in Chapter 2.

☐   The second type of site inspection takes place right at the end of the sales cycle. By that stage, a relationship has already been established between the venue and the prospect, following an enquiry being made and a proposal being sent out by the venue. A provisional booking may have been already made by the prospect, subject to their satisfaction with the final site inspection.

Regardless of which point in the sales cycle the site inspection visit takes place, the venue manager's prime objective should be not simply to show the venue to the visitor, but to attempt to get them to visualise how their event will work very well in the venue. But even before the visitor arrives for the site inspection, some preparation is necessary, to ensure its success.

Preparation for the site inspection

The person responsible for showing the visitor around should collect as much information as possible, in advance, about the types of events the visitor has held in the past – all of their events, not only the particular one they have in mind for their visit to the venue. That enables the venue manager to demonstrate how the venue could be used for the whole range of meetings that the prospect generally holds, not only for the particular event for which the prospect is seeking a venue.

It is essential that all concerned agree on the objectives and format of the visit. For example, it must be established in advance whether a visitor seeking a venue for a specific event prefers to have the site inspection before sitting down to discuss their event with the venue manager, or wishes to discuss their event before being shown around the venue. From the venue's perspective, the former format is often preferable, as it allows the person conducting the site inspection to more easily relate the tour to the specific event that the visitor has described.

Another important element of the format is the degree to which the visitor expects hospitality from the venue in terms of coffee or lunch. While almost every visitor will accept a cup of coffee before, during or after the site inspection, their expectations regarding lunch are often less clear. From the perspective of the venue manager, having lunch with the visitor provides a valuable opportunity to build the relationship that he or she already has with the prospect – an essential part of account development. It also allows for the gathering of more information about the prospect and their events.

But it should always be established in advance whether the visitor is free to accept the invitation to lunch at the venue. If they are, then it is essential that the venue representative allows sufficient time for this in their diary, as it leaves a poor impression if he or she needs to curtail the lunch in order to get back to their office or rush off to meet another prospect. If anyone has to rush off at the end of the lunch, it is far preferable that it is the visitor.

The final act of preparation for the site inspection should take place just before the visitor arrives, when the venue representative should take the tour themselves, in order to check, for example, that all areas are clean and tidy, lights are working, heating/cooling are turned on and the curtains are open. One venue manager learnt the hard way the importance of this pre-checking of the venue when, during a morning site inspection, he opened the door of a seminar room only to find that a homeless person had made it their sleeping accommodation for the previous night!

A comprehensive guide to what the visitor may focus on during their site inspection may be found in any of the numerous checklists available on the internet, designed to indicate to meetings and event planners exactly which features of the venue they should assess during their visit. Getting hold of one such checklist and ensuring in advance that all items listed are ready for inspection can be an effective way of getting the venue in order for visitors. One of the most complete checklists of this type is available free to download from www.write-style.co.uk

The visitor's arrival

First impressions count, and an effective site inspection begins right at the front door of the venue. It is worth remembering at all times that the prospect is paying the visit in order to find out if the venue is suitable for their event, and that they will consider the manner in which they are treated and greeted to be a reflection of what they can expect during their event.

The manner in which the visitor is welcomed can set the tone for the entire show-round. Therefore, the person or people working in the reception area of the venue should always be informed of the site inspection and the names of those attending. But it is even more impressive if the person conducting the site inspection is already in reception waiting to greet the visitor in person. At this point, body language is important, especially if this is the first time these people have met. A firm handshake and welcoming smile can build rapport by expressing a winning combination of confidence and warmth. Technology can also be harnessed to reinforce the message that the visitor is expected and their visit is important to the venue: if there are electronic screens in the reception area, a welcome message, with the company's logo, can be displayed on these.

In larger venues, with a more tiered management structure, it can be extremely useful if the General Manager or the Managing Director makes an appearance at the beginning of the site inspection – or indeed at any point – to greet the visitor. This is an effective way of demonstrating to the visitor that their interest in the venue is important to all of those employed there.

The classic question for visitors – 'did you find your way here easily?' – can be used as a way of engaging the visitor in a discussion of the venue's accessibility. If the visitor reports any particular challenges they encountered in finding their way to the venue (such as lack of signage or busy roads), this can spark a discussion of the best transport links leading to the venue, or how difficulties of orientation can be easily overcome by, for example, sending out information and maps to attendees.

Harnessing the visitor's imagination

An important challenge when showing visitors around an empty venue is succeeding in getting them to envisage their own event taking place there, thus making a valuable psychological connection between the venue and their own event. This entails prompting the visitor's imagination by walking them through the venue, following the actual journey that their own delegates would make and pointing out exactly how the visitor's event would work in the venue, from the registration area, meeting rooms and coffee break space, to the seminar rooms, restaurant, etc.

The visitor will be encouraged to envisage their own event taking place in the venue if, every step of the way, the venue representative gives an ongoing commentary along the lines of 'This is where you attendees will arrive. This is where they will have lunch. This is where their break-out sessions will take place ...'

If possible, rooms should be furnished as they would be for an event similar to that which the visitor is planning, so that they are not simply looking at empty spaces. The visitor's logo displayed on the screen in the auditorium is another useful touch – which adds to the overall image of the meeting room. If rooms are already in use by clients on the day of the site inspection, it is important to inform the visitor in advance that some rooms will not be available for viewing. However, it may be possible to look briefly into a room in use by another client if that client's relationship with the venue allows this. If that is the case, seeing the rooms set up and full of attendees, can help the client visualise their own event in the same rooms.

Dealing with objections

At regular intervals throughout the site inspection, it is advisable to solicit feedback from the visitor, on what they think of the venue so far. It is also good policy to invite the visitor to openly express any objections they may have. This lowers the possibility of the prospect leaving with unexpressed concerns or mistaken impressions. By proactively soliciting feedback as the site inspection proceeds, the venue representative gets the opportunity to answer any points raised.

Objections should be anticipated and dealt with convincingly. For example, if the visitor comments that there is a long walk from the entrance to the meeting room, or that attendees may experience problems of orientation between meeting rooms, this can be countered by a description of how the venue will strive to provide solutions. In the case of the visitor raising concerns about their attendees encountering potential problems when navigating their way around the venue, it can be suggested that the venue will provide extra directional signage or human signage, and that the event organiser's logo can be displayed on signage, to help boost their branding, for example.

Being shown meeting rooms with no natural daylight can be another common reason for the visitor to raise an objection. This is more challenging for the venue representative to deal with, but he or she can respond by asking the visitor why natural daylight is important to them. How long will they actually be in the windowless room? It may be possible to convince them that having no natural daylight in a room that is only going to be used for the opening and closing plenary sessions, for example, is not as much of a disadvantage as it may initially appear to be.

Managing the site inspection conversation

As an essential part of the sales process, the site inspection provides the venue representative with the opportunity to promote the venue's advantages during the conversation that takes place as he or she walks along with the visitor. Story-telling is the key to maintaining the visitor's interest while at the same time selling the venue's strong points to them. Those stories can bring the venue to life by, for example, focusing on its unique history and 'personality'. It is also important to mention the names of other clients who have already used the venue successfully. Why did they use the venue and how did they use it? In order to facilitate this, i-Pads can be used to show photographs of rooms as they were decorated and configured for use by previous clients of the venue.

The site inspection conversation should always return, from time to time, to how the venue closely aligns with the objectives of the visitor's planned event. Therefore, the more the venue representative already knows about the visitor's event – its objectives, format, the profile of the attendees, and so on – the more likely they are to be able to do this successfully. And it is not always necessary to simply accept the visitor's own ideas for how their event will be run – the visitor may welcome other possible solutions. For example, the venue manager may be able to suggest to the prospect a format or set-up for their event that would work more effectively than the one they have in mind. Most prospects are grateful for this type of suggestion.

A legitimate question that may also be asked of the site inspection visitor is: what other venues are they visiting or considering for their event? The answer to that question (assuming an answer is given –

which may not be the case) enables the venue representative to make comparisons between their venue and the others being considered by the prospect – although the temptation to be negative about competing venues should always be resisted.

The level of the conversation will differ according to whether the person being shown the venue is experienced or inexperienced in the art of planning meetings and choosing venues for their events. For that reason, the venue representative must judge, at an early stage, just how much experience the visitor already has in this field. An inexperienced prospect, for example, may not have even considered the format that their event will take or the set-up of the event. In such cases, the venue representative will need to offer guidance and suggestions as to what will work best. There is much less need to go into basic details of this type with experienced meetings planners, who are much more likely to have a clear idea of what it is they are looking for, from a venue.

At times, other members of the venue staff may be invited to join the conversation and provide answers on their particular specialist role. For example, if the site inspection includes a visit to the banqueting area, it can be useful if the banqueting manager is there to greet the visitor and answer any specific food and beverage enquiries. Similarly, a discussion with the person responsible for the venue's audio-visual facilities can also be helpful to visitors with questions or concerns about that aspect of their event. Again, it is important to establish prior to the site inspection what elements need to be discussed so the appropriate people can be asked to meet with the prospect at some stage of their visit. Nevertheless, the venue representative should be knowledgeable enough to conduct the site inspection to a fairly detailed standard and to answer the majority of the prospect's questions.

Site inspections as part of familiarisation trips and press trips

The familiarisation ('fam') trips were discussed in Chapter 4 in the context of CVBs. When a fam trip includes a number of site inspections, the visitors tend to arrive at the venue in large groups of up to twenty people. This size of group is too large to be shown around by only one person, so it is vital that sufficient numbers of venue staff are available to ensure that the group can be divided into smaller groups of 5 or 6 people. The Canberra Convention Bureau's guidance to the city's venues on conducting site inspections for fam trip groups includes the following piece of advice:

> With larger groups we recommend you do not talk as you walk in the way you would normally do if showing two of three people your property. Walk the group into a room, wait and allow them to assemble and then present – this ensures the people at the back of the group do not miss any of the important information (Canberra CB, 2010)

The principles for preparing for such visits are similar to the preparation carried out by the venue for one visitor. It is essential to find out in advance who is in the group and what type of events they organise. This avoids the mistake of, for example, wasting the visitors' time by showing them rooms that are too large or too small for their events.

Bearing in mind that fam trips can include three or four site inspections on the same day, it is best for venue managers, if possible, to arrange with the fam trip organisers for their venue to be the first venue of the day, as participants will still be fresh and not yet saturated with information and impressions. They are also less likely to be running late, if the site inspection takes place early in their programme for that day. If the venue being visited is not the first site inspection of the day, then it is important to find out where the fam trip group has already been and to take into account how tired they are likely to be. If their time is very limited or they are clearly exhausted, it could be better to simply offer the fam trip participants drinks and a short presentation, rather than walking them through the whole venue, especially if the venue is large – and then follow-up afterwards.

A drinks reception after the site inspection gives the individuals in the fam trip group the opportunity to interact on a one-to-one basis with members of the venue's management team, and ask questions. It is also a chance for the venue staff to get to know the prospects better.

Site inspections for journalists need to be handled differently, as the visitors' objectives are not the same as those of meeting planners. Journalists want to hear about and see something new – for example a refurbishment or extension to the venue, or newly-installed videoconferencing facilities, rather than technical details and prices. In effect, they are coming to interview the venue representative, for their article. The venue representative needs to be prepared for that, and ready with answers including appropriate facts and figures.

Ending the site inspection

Last impressions count as much as first impressions, and for that reason, the end of the site inspection should be planned as meticulously as the beginning. As the visit draws to a close, it is reasonable to ask the visitors for feedback on what they have seen. This may generate additional objections – which should be dealt with as they arise. It is also important to agree with the visitor what kind of follow-up actions will be taken, after the site inspection.

Many venues offer visitors some form of collateral in the form of information folders or brochures to take away with them. But these can be cumbersome to carry around, especially the recipient has other site inspections to do on the same day. An alternative take-away would be a gift of a memory stick, with relevant venue information pre-loaded on to it.

But in any case, it is essential that the prospect is given all the details of the venue that they require in order to make an informed decision as to its suitability for their event. A follow-up email with all of the information relevant to the conversations that have taken place during the site inspection gives the venue manager an opportunity to make contact with the prospect again and to move them forward in the sales process.

The Royal Institute of British Architects (RIBA Venues), London: The Experience Show-round

Offering an 'Experience Show-round' to potential clients, demonstrating a full event experience and highlighting the venue's many architectural features.

The Venue

The Royal Institute of British Architects (RIBA), with its headquarters at 66 Portland Place, London, was founded in 1834 and after moving three times, settled in the current location a century later. The six-storey building, designed by George Grey Wornum in an art-deco and modernist style, was opened on 8 November 1934 by King George V and Queen Mary. The building's unique architectural features make it an interesting backdrop for filming period productions, and for that reason the venue has featured in a number of TV and movie scenes.

The RIBA was not only built for 'the advancement of architecture and the knowledge of the arts and sciences connected therewith' but also as a meeting, learning and exhibition space for its 42,000 members. The venue offers 24 meeting facilities, ranging from breakout rooms for eight guests to an auditorium seating 400 delegates.

5

First impressions are important

Its central location, spectacular views over London's skyline, its architecture and rotating cultural exhibitions offer an exciting backdrop for conferences, meetings, dinners, receptions, birthdays and weddings all year round.

The contemporary meeting rooms on the upper floors overlooking London, as well as the traditional boardrooms with leather-lined walls accommodate events from a broad range of markets.

By day, the 400-seater Jarvis Auditorium and the Florence Hall with its high ceilings and vast windows accommodate large conferences and exhibitions; and by night the Florence Hall is open for evening events.

With three roof terraces, the RIBA venue is also one of the rare venues in London with extensive outside space, which makes it very popular for barbecues and 'sundowner' receptions on summer evenings.

The Clients

Due to RIBA's versatile venue spaces, its marketing focus is widely spread between private, corporate, association markets and charities. As a result, the RIBA venues host approximately 2,400 events per year attended by around 74,000 attendees from the United Kingdom and overseas. The principal market segments are:

■   Construction, architecture, designer and creative companies that use the venue for their meetings, awards ceremonies and exhibitions, due to the building's architectural importance and its association with the representing body for architecture in the United Kingdom and the world.

■   Cultural, financial and educational organisations, as well as environmental enterprises attracted by the RIBA's green reputation and commitment to sustainability.

■   Media, marketing and advertising companies, many of which have their head offices in close proximity to the venue and find it a convenient location for their conferences and product launches.

■   Charities. Being a charity itself, the RIBA has hosted numerous other charities' events over the years from fundraising dinners to childrens' playground activities.

■   Special events from weddings and bar mitzvahs to birthday parties, particularly at weekends. Letting out the event spaces to the general public for these purposes not only opens up the venue to a wider audience, but also further contributes to generating revenue, which in turn helps to fund the many important activities the RIBA charity is involved in.

Overall, the venue prides itself on the large proportion of repeat business they receive each year and their longstanding client base of international corporate clients.

The Experience Show-round

In the attempt to gain the competitive edge, and taking into account the fact that a common pre-conceived concern of new prospects is 'What could architects possibly know about how to run an event?', it became a priority to demonstrate the full event experience to the client at the first opportunity – the show-round.

There is a widely-held belief among venue sales staff that the main objective of a show-round is simply to show the prospect around the appropriate rooms, mention any other relevant facilities, and perhaps offer a coffee or tea before releasing the potential client to go about their usual business.

The sales team at the RIBA realised that presenting any venue in that manner has been rendered obsolete due to meeting room images, 360-degree videos and layout plans now being accessible on the venue's website for clients to view. So the challenge was to find a way to make a show-round more attractive and worthwhile for the event organiser taking the time to visit the venue.

5

To add real value to a show-round and create an experience, the RIBA team identified the following four guidelines as valuable additions to the basic site-inspection:

1. To design all aspects of the show-round as an event

At the RIBA, a specific time-frame and location for the show-round is agreed and the organiser receives a written confirmation of the appointment. This way, sufficient time is allocated by the prospect and the sales staff to conduct a full show-round experience. On average, a minimum of one hour is allocated to the show-round.

The sales team reserves all rooms to be included in the show-round in the venue's booking system, with the desired set up and amenities. Other key rooms, which are not part of the event enquiry are also reserved, so that the prospect can acquire a full impression of the venue's versatile facilities and its potential.

Refreshments are pre-ordered to showcase the quality of catering available at the venue. Offering refreshments in an actual meeting room rather than in a public area allows the prospect to experience the event space for longer and discuss specific features of the room and its unique selling points while enjoying a cup of coffee.

In addition, the sales person organises a PowerPoint presentation or video of the venue to be shown during the site inspection in order to demonstrate the audio visual facilities available and their quality. Other amenities which are part of the venue's standard offer are also provided in the rooms to paint a complete picture of how the rooms would look on the day of the client's event.

Treating the visit as an event in this way, not only guarantees that all facilities and services clearly reflect the professional standard of the venue but also ensures that all front of house staff are aware of the show-round and its importance.

2. To follow the attendee's journey

The prospect is walked and talked through the delegate journey of their event, which starts at the entrance and includes all facilities the event may include, for example parking, cloakroom facilities, registration area, etc.

Following and explaining the path of the event's attendees brings the venue alive and enables the prospect to visualise the day's proceedings. In addition, the sales person shows images of similar events on an i-Pad to the organiser and discusses the full potential of the event space.

While walking along the customer journey, the event organiser is more likely to ask questions about the logistics of the event, and any specific requirements can be addressed and discussed by the venue staff, there and then. The prospect is then prompted to consider all aspects of organising an event in conjunction with the venue's offer.

The journey is likewise used by the venue to introduce key event staff to the prospect (e.g. head chef, operations manager and audio visual manager), which further allows the prospect to become aware of the venue's ethos and professionalism.

3. To tell a story

'Everybody loves a good story!'

In order to add uniqueness and a lasting impression to the show-round, the sales person endeavours to strike a good balance between event-related information and interesting facts about the venue. Stories about the origin of the venue, historical facts, famous guests, and extraordinary features are added to the show-round experience to make a stronger impression and keep the venue in the prospect's memory for longer.

The information, facts and stories about the RIBA were gathered by the venue's team from two main sources – first from consulting the RIBA's archives and second from the knowledge of long-serving members of staff. These supply venue sales staff with a wealth of useful anecdotes, unusual facts and personal insights. The phrase 'Did you know....?' is often used by the sales team to start an anecdote. For example: 'Did you know about the mystery of our First World War memorial inscription at the RIBA? One architect's name is blanked out on the memorial, as it was later discovered that he actually was very much alive and hadn't died in the war!'

The venue team believes that if the prospect repeats some of these newly-learnt facts to colleagues and friends, this can add to the RIBA's exposure and create further interest for the venue. The stories can also be used by the organiser in delegate material and invitations to create further excitement about the venue prior to the event.

In addition, learning about facts which are not widely known or published makes the client feel special and privileged. Being given this type of 'inside' information about the venue can lead to the prospect building a stronger bond with the venue. And highlighting unique features of the building helps make the walls come alive and imprints an exciting image in the prospect's memory.

4. To bond with the client

5

The venue's team not only showcases the facilities, services and people at RIBA but also uses the time to bond with the event organiser. 'People buy people' is a well-known human factor that affects the decision-making process in many purchasing situations.

Building the base for a long-lasting relationship with the prospect during the first face-to-face contact is considered to be the most important part of the show-round in terms of helping RIBA staff secure the business.

At the venue, the client is met by a professionally-dressed sales person with a smile and welcoming body language. By asking questions, listening well and paying full attention throughout the show-round, the venue's team member demonstrates their interest in the event and in the person.

The natural and humane approach of the sales person builds trust and confidence in the venue and the prospect feels that they and their event are in safe hands.

After the details of the event have been discussed and while the refreshments are being served, the sales person uses the time for a casual chat with the prospect to establish a common interest and to find out what is important to them. This information is then used in future correspondence with the client to strengthen and prolong the relationship.

The result

The RIBA venues team collects feedback via a third party from all event organisers after the event. Since the introduction of the Experience Show-round, the positive feedback for the venue's "Pre-event communication" increased by 21%.

In addition, the sales team have received frequent 'thank- you' e-mails from prospects, enthusing about the show-round, which the team had not received before. For example:

'BLM is a member of the RIBA panel of legal advisors and I have a personal interest in architecture, so I had high hopes for my site visit to RIBA. Thankfully the experience lived up to expectations – I received a warm and professional welcome and a thorough tour of their beautiful conference spaces. Maria was very helpful in setting up the visit and knowledgeable in the show-round, explaining both the history and features of the rooms on offer. She helped me to visualise how the event spaces would work for our particular needs, and I was also able to meet the AV manager which was useful. I left feeling very optimistic and I am sure that we will be running some great events at RIBA soon.'

'Just a quick note to say that it was very good to meet you and Vicky this morning.

Thank you very much for taking time out to show me around the RIBA. It is a wonderful event space and venue and I especially enjoyed our chat about Greece and the delicious home-baked cookies'.

'Thank you so much for showing me around yesterday. I can understand your enthusiasm working for RIBA, having seen how interesting the building is. I can't wait to use RIBA for our next meeting….'

'Thank you for your time earlier. It was a pleasure meeting you at such short notice. My visit to the RIBA was completely above and beyond what I had expected and I will treasure the olive oil bottle with herbs from your gardens for a long time'.

Even though the success of a prospect show-round is not always tangible or easily measured due to the visit being held at an early stage in the venue selection process, this valuable opportunity to make a strong first impression is not to be missed.

RIBA Venues show-round procedure

Prior

- E-mail confirmation of show-round and schedule at least 1 hour of client's time, if possible 3 days prior to the appointment

- Book the function room(s), layout and catering (hospitality tray), and AV presentation inside the room(s) (as if a normal booking) with "SHOW" status.

On the day

- Check room(s) prior to arrival of guest that they are lit, clean and correctly set up (no unclothed catering tables!!). Also check that catering and AV is set up as requested

- Check the availability of other the key rooms in case you get the opportunity to upsell for future events (Florence, Jarvis, Aston Webb, Lutyens, Wren, Nash)

- Be ready when client arrives and reception calls

- Meet client in the entrance hall (less than 5mins after the call)

- Take factsheet and iPad with you for reference

- Point out 2-5 features in entrance hall (from factsheet)

- (e.g. doors, left and right inscriptions, Wornum bust, one of the floor inscriptions)

- Explain the customer journey/how guests arrive on the day of the event (reception is manned, cloakroom etc…)

- If appropriate walk client to cloakroom and toilets downstairs, point out 2 features on the staircase (e.g. King George V inscription, Lions- what they stand for)

- Walk to 1st floor before taking the lift to showcase the grand staircase, explain building structure and fabrics (e.g. wood, glass, four columns with black Ashburton marble, etc)

- Point out at 1-3 other features on the way to the room (e.g. wooden panelling, Aston Webb, exhibition Gallery 1)

- Entrance area to the room, explain what it could be used for (e.g. refreshments, registration etc.)

- Enter room(s) and point out at least 3 features of the room (e.g. views, architecture, layouts etc.)

- Discuss event details and offer additional options

- Sit down with client and have tea, coffee and hospitality tray inside the room and find common ground and interests

Questions

■ Event details? Take notes on function sheet

■ What is important to them?

■ Where else was the event held before?

■ What other events do they organise?

■ What other rooms might be suitable?

■ Chat about things/interests you and the organiser have in common

■ Summarise the details as discussed so far (paint a picture of event)

■ Ask: "Would these arrangements work for your event?"

■ Address any concerns if given or ask when the decision will be made and by whom

Complete the show-round

■ Walk down the staircase to the entrance with the guest and show any other rooms on the way they might be interested in (for the same event or other future events)

■ Say good bye at the door with a firm handshake and advise the guest that you will send a follow up e-mail with all details discussed in the next two days.

After the show-round

■ Send follow up e-mail to thank them for their time, with any outstanding information they required during the show-round

■ E-mail updated proposal letter and resend terms & conditions. Remind them to sign the contract within the specified time

■ CALL client to chase for signed contract as applicable

Salzburg Sheraton - The power of personalizing site inspections and going the extra mile

The venue

Sheraton Salzburg Hotel (http://www.sheratonsalzburg.com/) is located in the city centre, with 166 guest rooms and suites, 3 permanent function rooms and direct connection to the Salzburg Congress Centre (for which the Sheraton is the exclusive catering partner). The hotel is located 15 minutes' drive from Salzburg airport and 5 minutes' drive from the central station.

The Salzburg Sheraton, photo courtesy Sheraton Hotels

The client

The client was a major designer and manufacturer of clothing and accessories.

The event

An annual meeting of major retail partners and brand representatives involved in the distribution of the client's merchandise. The business potential of this event was a booking of more than 135 single rooms for 4 nights, including the use of the hotel's function rooms together with selected rooms at the Salzburg Congress Centre. In addition to providing such a high volume of business, it is important to note that this event was scheduled to take place during the low season in terms of demand for hotel facilities in Salzburg.

The competition

Following the call for proposals and subsequent shortlisting, three Salzburg hotels were left pitching for this event. As well as the Sheraton, there were two other properties - both 4-star hotels, and both equipped with more meetings rooms and more bedrooms than the Sheraton: 190 and 220 bedrooms compared with the Sheraton's 166. In addition, the Sheraton was at a disadvantage regarding prices when compared with these competing hotels, as the cost of hiring meeting rooms in the Congress Centre is much higher than choosing a hotel that provides all of the required function space onsite. Furthermore, the Sheraton's bedroom rates were approximately 15-20% higher than those of the other two hotels pitching for this event.

On the other hand, in terms of the physical condition of these three properties, one of the other hotels in the competition was in need of refurbishment, and was scheduled to close for this purpose two months after the date of this event. However, the Sheraton's other competitor had been fully refurbished only two years previously and was therefore in excellent condition. The Sheraton itself had been in the process of undergoing a complete refurbishment, with only two levels (out of seven) and some public areas left to be completed. Therefore, in terms of the hotels' respective physical conditions, the Sheraton was neither at the greatest advantage or the least.

The site visit

The three hotels selected as potential venues for this event were visited by the client in June 2013, five months before the date of the actual event. Stefan Pils, Sales Representative at Starwood Hotels & Resorts Worldwide Inc. representing the Sheraton Salzburg Hotel, describes how the site inspection was planned and executed:

During one of the regular morning meetings of our sales team, when new inquiries and the progress of existing inquiries are discussed, we realized that this event, worth over 520 room nights during a low period of demand, from a client who was new to us, was one that we simply had to win!

Once the date for the site inspection had been agreed, we knew that we had a mission to accomplish. Fortunately, we had already developed a set of internal guidelines we called 'The power of the site inspection', designed to set the highest standards for tours through our property. These guidelines include:

- Checking the condition of all rooms to be shown (letting in some fresh air, switching on lights and TV, and checking for cleanliness)

- Arranging for our General Manager to welcome the prospect in the lobby

- Preparing giveaways (usually a bag with detailed information on the hotel, together with some handmade chocolate pralines, a confectionary closely associated with Salzburg)

- Reserving a table in our Club Lounge for coffee with the prospect after the site inspection

- Keeping some space free in front of the hotel for the prospects to park their cars

- Being in the lobby 5 minutes before the time of the appointment with the prospect.

None of these common-sense measures may seem particularly significant in itself, but we were aware that it was those small details that could make all the difference to the success rate of our site inspections, and, for that reason, we considered it necessary to write them down in the form of a list available to all staff doing site inspections of our venue.

Even the chocolate pralines were important! Knowing that prospects can only absorb a certain amount of technical details throughout their visit, we put the pralines in the bag along with the factsheet on the venue's facilities and services as an incentive for the prospect to open the bag afterwards and enjoy the confectionary while reading the factsheet.

Our 'Power of the site inspection' guidelines are constantly evolving as we continuously try to improve our performance in this aspect of our work by using our own creativity as well as new ideas taken from other venues. However, we are aware that the most important element in persuading potential clients to choose our venue is personalization. For example, putting the prospect's logo, merchandising and corporate design on every available display in our venue during their visit, helps give them the impression that they are already experiencing that event taking place in our venue, as opposed to simply being at the beginning of the planning stage.

In the case of this particular site inspection, our personalization efforts began by us displaying the prospect's logo on the meeting room board in our lobby, which usually lists the clients who are holding events in our venue on any particular day.

This immediately came to the prospects' attention as they entered the hotel. We also put their logo on the electronic display outside every meeting room that day, and had the same logo projected on to the screens inside each meeting room. Crucially, we had each meeting room's seating configured according to how it would look during the prospects' actual meeting.

The Papageno Meeting room, photo courtesy Sheraton Hotels

Moving on to the bedrooms, we made sure that placed on the bed of each room to be visited there was one of the prospect's own branded shopping bags together with one of our Sheraton bags. Those bags were filled with various items to make it look as though the room was occupied by a guest who had just came back from visiting one of the prospect's shops. The image of our Sheraton brand next to theirs on the two shopping bags was designed to create a feeling of connection between the prospect and ourselves.

As preparation for every meeting I always try to find out as many details as possible, on the prospect's business. In this case, in addition to familiarizing myself with the company's history, owners, business partners and main competitors, I discovered their slogan 'Long Live Vintage'. I made reference to this on several occasions during the site visit, when, for example, showing the prospect a room decorated with antique pictures.

In the ten minutes remaining at the end of our tour in the prospects' strict schedule, we had just enough time left for a cup of coffee. It is important to note that ours was the first venue of the three being visited on that day, which can at times be a disadvantage in terms of the limitation on the time allocated before the prospect has to move on to the next venue. However, we made the most of those last ten minutes in order to leave a positive impression in the prospects' minds after they left us. As we sat down for coffee, our Food and Beverage Manager arrived and presented the prospects with a cake, made by our own patisserie and decorated with a small watch and handbag made out of marzipan. Watches and handbags are two of the prospect's most popular products, and their obvious delight at receiving this gift told us that we had been right to make this final gesture.

When the visitors were leaving, we offered to look after their cars for the rest of the day, as they would be able to reach the other two venues by foot from our hotel. They agreed, but before we let them go we gave them some bottled water to take away with them and invited them to have lunch with us if they had any free time around noon. They declined this offer, but seemed grateful for the gesture.

Later that day, when the concierge called to tell me that the prospects had returned to pick up their cars, I went to meet them and handed over another cake for their colleagues back at their office. Through this final gesture, I believe that we achieved something very important in the sense that our venue (and I myself) constituted their last impressions before leaving our city.

Four days later, we received the news that our venue had been chosen for this event, and it was made clear to us that a major factor in the client's decision had been the personalized touch that we had demonstrated throughout the site inspection.

The lesson is clear: if the prospect is willing to visit your venue, do as much as you can in order to persuade them that your property is the perfect match with their event. A site inspection offers you a golden opportunity to differentiate yourself from the competition, and personalizing the visit and making it as memorable as possible is one of the most effective ways of doing this. In my experience, the site inspection, as a sales tool, is greatly underestimated by many venues, who simply do their standard, off-the-peg tour, with only one result: a bored prospect. Our site inspections at the Salzburg Sheraton have brought us a number of major event bookings, even on occasions such as in the above example when our rates were higher than those of our competitors and our competitors' facilities were in some ways more suitable to the client's needs. Never underestimate the power of the site inspection.

5

Further reading

Canberra CB (2010*), How to run a site inspection for Canberra Convention Bureau Familiarisations* available from http://www.canberraconvention.com.au

Online sources of further information

Write Style Communications Ltd: Fam Trips, Site Visits Site Inspections Handbook and Checklist
www.write-style.co.uk/7.html

David Brudney & Associates: Site Inspections - New Generation of Hospitality Sales Professionals
www.davidbrudney.com/articles/2007-mar-site-inspections.php

MeetingsNet: Great Moments in Site Inspections
http://meetingsnet.com/site-selectionrfps/great-moments-site-inspections

How to run a site inspection for familiarisation trip groups, Canberra Convention Bureau.
www.canberraconvention.com.au/pages/page215.asp

6 Winning New Business at Exhibitions

Exhibition visitors

Exhibitions are a form of modern-day marketplace that offer venue sales staff an extremely valuable face-to-face selling opportunity with a self-selected audience. They may be considered 'self-selected', because the visitors to these business events have voluntarily chosen to attend, having a specific interest in the facilities, services or products being presented at the exhibition. From the point of view of venue sales staff, specialist exhibitions provide an environment in which they can meet prospects face-to-face and put into use the qualifying skills discussed in Chapter 2.

Those exhibitions which attract visitors who are potential customers for venues are generally business-to-business (B2B) events where facilities and services that support the meetings industry are to be found promoting themselves to visitors. At such events, venues find themselves exhibiting alongside a wide range of organisations and suppliers such as convention bureaus, hotels and other accommodation providers, transport companies, audio-visual services and interpreters, as well as manufacturers/distributors of meetings-related merchandise ranging from delegate badges to conference bags.

The visitors to these exhibitions are in general people with a specialist interest in acquiring knowledge of the facilities, services and products that are presented on the exhibition stands and which they need to be familiar with in order to effectively carry out their professional duties. Although exhibition visitors include a wide range of professionals including meetings industry journalists, specialist consultants, as well as academics and students specialising in events management or business tourism, the majority of visitors – and those clearly of most interest to exhibitors – are people whose professional role includes the planning and running of meetings and events. For these visitors, exhibitions are an opportunity to keep up to date with the supply of destinations and venues that may serve as the locations for the events they organise. They attend seeking information, ideas and suggestions for their future events, as well as the chance to meet and engage with the professionals charged with attracting clients to their venues.

At many meetings industry exhibitions, certain visitors are 'hosted buyers' who have been qualified by the exhibition organisers as valuable, bona fide, meetings planners actively seeking destinations and venues for their events. The travel and accommodation expenses they incur in attending the show are paid by the exhibition organisers – funded from the fees that the exhibitors pay to the organisers. In return for their expenses being paid in this way, the hosted buyers are obliged to attend a certain number of appointments with exhibitors. They may choose which exhibitors they wish to meet according to the profiles provided by exhibitors in the show catalogue; but exhibitors can also request appointments with those hosted buyers whom they have specifically identified as potential clients. These appointments may take the form of one-to-one meetings between exhibitors and hosted buyers or presentations made by exhibitors to groups of hosted buyers, on the stand. When venues exhibit as part of a stand managed by their convention bureau, group presentations are generally given by the relevant convention bureau rather than individual venues – see below: 'Partnering with Convention Bureaus'. But when venues manage their own individual and independent stand, they can – and do – make their own presentations to groups of hosted buyers.

How can venues make the most of this unique opportunity that exhibitions create by bringing them face-to-face with large numbers of potential customers?

Choosing where to exhibit

While some general travel and tourism exhibitions may have a particular section of the show – or a particular day of the event – on a meetings industry theme, there are a significant, and growing, number of annual, specialist exhibitions that are wholly and exclusively dedicated to the meetings industry.

These may be classified in several ways. One way of doing so is according to the specific type of venue exhibiting. There are specialist, niche, exhibitions at which only one type of venue is represented. A well-established example is the Academic Venue Show in London, for university- and college-based venues in the United Kingdom. Similarly, at shows such as the International Luxury Travel Market in Cannes, highly prestigious venues such as converted castles, palaces and monasteries are among the exhibitors.

But the most commonly-found system of categorising meetings industry exhibitions is in terms of the geographical markets they aim to cover. A few, such as EIBTM in Barcelona and IMEX in Frankfurt cover the global meetings industry market, attracting exhibitors and visitors from countries worldwide. Others focus upon a particular world region: AIME in Melbourne, for example, covers Australia and South-East Asia; GIBTM in Abu Dhabi covers the Middle East; and Convene, in Vilnius, targets the Baltic Sea Region. Many shows have a national spread of exhibitors: Salon Bedouk in Paris, for instance, attracts exhibitors from all over France; and BTC in Florence is largely aimed at the Italian market. Finally, some exhibitions for the meetings industry have a sub-national, regional focus. An example of such an event would be the German exhibition, Locations, which takes place each year in four cities, each one situated in a different region of Germany: Rhein-Neckar, Stuttgart Region, Rhein-Ruhr and Rhein-Main.

Figure 6.1 shows the main meetings industry exhibitions and the markets upon which they focus.

EXHIBITION	FOCUS	LOCATION	WEBSITE
Best of Events	Germany	Dortmund	www.bo-e.de
Conventa	Southeast Europe	Ljubljana	www.conventa.si
EMITT	Turkey	Istanbul	www.emittistanbul.com/en
FITUR	Spain, Southern Europe	Madrid	www.ifema.es/fitur_06
Salon Bedouk	France	Paris	www.salon.bedouk.com
MCE CEE	Central, Eastern Europe	Budapest	www.europecongress.com
Convene	Baltics	Vilnius	www.convene.lt
BIT	Italy	Milan	www.bit.fieramilano.it/en
Meetings Africa	South Africa	Johannesburg	www.meetingsafrica.co.za
AIME	Australia, Southeast Asia	Melbourne	www.aime.com.au
Business & Meeting Solutions	Belgium, Benelux	Brussels	www.business-meeting-solutions.com
DMAI	US	Washington	www.destinationsshowcase.com
International Confex	UK, International	London	www.international-confex.com
MITT	Russia	Moscow	www.mitt.ru/en
GIBTM	Gulf	Abu Dhabi	www.gibtm.com
UITT	Ukraine	Kiev	www.uitt-kiev.com/en
IT&CM China	China	Shanghai	www.itcmchina.com
IMEX	International	Frankfurt	www.imex-frankfurt.com
AIBTM	US, International	Orlando	www.aibtm.com
IT&CM India	India	Delhi	www.itcmindia.com
SuisseEMEX	Switzerland	Zurich	www.suisse-emex.ch
CIBTM	China	Beijing	www.cibtm.com
IT&CMA	Asia	Bangkok	www.itcma.com
IMEX America	US, International	Las Vegas	www.imex-america.com
BTC	Italy	Florence	www.btc.it
EIBTM	International	Barcelona	www.eibtm.com
MBT Market	Germany	Munich	www.mbt-market.de
The Meetings Show	UK, International	London	www.themeetingsshow.com
Square Meal Venues and Events	UK	London	www.venuesandevents.co.uk

Figure 6.1: Meetings Industry Exhibitions, According to Geographical Market. Adapted from Conference & Incentive Management magazine, Issue 6, November 2012

Most of the international exhibitions are 'destination-led', in the sense that the stands are arranged in zones according to world region. Given the fact that, in most cases, meeting planners choose destinations before venues, this zone system simplifies the task of exhibition visitors, who can more easily navigate their way around the show and find venues and other suppliers in the regions that they use – or may use in the future – for their meetings and events. It also determines where any particular venue will be logically located at the exhibition.

But whatever the size or location of the exhibition, the cost of exhibiting represents a significant investment for any venue, taking into account the expense incurred in hiring exhibition space, staff transport and accommodation, insurance and on-stand literature, as well as the design, construction, storage and transportation of the stand itself. To these outlays must be added the opportunity costs of key members of staff being absent from their place of work and their other duties. A balance must be struck between the need to have sufficient numbers of venue staff on the stand and not neglecting the work to be done back in the office.

For these reasons, it is rare to find venues that can afford to exhibit at more than three or four exhibitions each year. Many are limited to one only, so the choice of where to exhibit is a major consideration for any venue manager.

6

The decision of where to exhibit must essentially be based on the venue's sales and marketing strategy and, more specifically, the budget available and the geographical segment of the market that is being targeted by the venue. Thus, it would make sense for a venue that, for example due to its size or location, was seeking to attract domestic clients to invest in exhibiting at a national or regional exhibition first and foremost.

In general, the manager in the venue who has responsibility for choosing where to exhibit must gather as much information as possible about the exhibition in advance of deciding whether or not to invest in exhibiting there. These days, exhibition attendance is usually audited by an independent body to avoid the organisers making exaggerated claims about the number and nature of the visitors who attend. The auditors' data – usually supplied on request from the exhibition organisers

– should not only give a reasonably accurate estimate of the numbers of visitors attending each year, but also breakdown of their profile in terms of level of responsibility for making purchasing decisions and their spending power, as well as details of any hosted buyer system in place.

Data such as this, however, can reveal only a partial picture of any exhibition, and many venue managers would wish to supplement their analysis of the information supplied by the exhibition organisers by first of all attending, as a visitor, any show at which they were considering exhibiting. A walk around the stands at the show will quickly reveal the extent to which there is the vital 'buzz' that comes from exhibitors interacting with visitors to their mutual benefit and that denotes a successful event. Discreet discussions with exhibitors can help determine how satisfied they are with the volume and value of the visitors they have met, as well as with the general planning, logistics and marketing of the exhibition, undertaken by the organisers.

Choosing how to exhibit

Having decided to exhibit, an early decision facing any venue is whether to share a stand with other exhibitors, or to have its own stand, entirely independent of others. Each system offers its own particular benefits.

■ Partnering with convention bureaus

A tried-and-tested solution is for a venue to share a stand with other suppliers from the same destination under the umbrella of their local or national convention bureau. As previously mentioned, large international exhibitions for the meetings industry are destination-led and arranged according to individual continents and countries. Therefore a meeting planner interested in organising an event in, for example, Poland, will tend to seek out the exhibition stand of the Poland convention bureau, where they will expect to find representatives from the principal Polish cities' convention bureaus, venues located in those cities, as well as other suppliers such as DMCs, sharing the stand space.

Apart from the benefit of being easily located by visitors, venues may enjoy several additional advantages in sharing a stand with their relevant convention bureau:

1   The cost will generally be lower than exhibiting independently, as the expense incurred in the design, transportation, construction and storage of the stand, as well as the hiring of the exhibiting space, will be shared among several exhibitors.

2   Venues benefit from any investment that the convention bureau makes in terms of pre-exhibition promotion to attract visitors to the stand.

3   Venues benefit from the extra visitation on the stand created by any events (receptions, 'happy-hours', cocktails, etc.) organised by the convention bureau (but possibly *sponsored* by an exhibiting venue, bringing the venue additional brand exposure).

4   Exposure to the hosted buyers groups that come to the stand to attend presentations given by the convention bureau. Although these presentations are generally destination-focused, there can sometimes be the opportunity for venue managers to have a slot within the overall presentation, to introduce themselves and their facility. Many convention bureaus also provide lunch on the stand for their hosted buyers groups, and that gives the venue managers a further opportunity to mingle and network with these important prospects.

6

■ Partnering with members of an association or marketing consortium

For those venues that are members of a venue-only association or marketing consortium, an alternative is to share a stand with other venues, under the umbrella of that organisation. For example, at a number of large meetings industry exhibitions, the Historic Conference Centres of Europe marketing consortium (www.hcce.com) hires a stand for its members – venues located in historic buildings such as monasteries and opera houses.

The advantages, to venues, of exhibiting in this way are similar to those described above for exhibiting in partnership with a Convention Bureau. One disadvantage, however, is that the venue's link, at the exhibition, to the specific country in which it is located is broken, as international marketing consortia, by definition, include members from a number of different countries.

■   Having a separate stand

An alternative to sharing a stand with other suppliers, under the umbrella of the convention bureau, marketing consortium or association is for venues to go it alone by having an independent stand, exclusively for their facility. Most venues, however, would resist opting for this method of exhibiting in the case of major international meetings industry exhibitions, in order to benefit from the advantages of partnering with convention bureaus, as listed above. They may also wish to avoid the possibility of being dwarfed by the large stands that tend to dominate such events. In addition, the cost of hiring stand space exclusively for one venue could be prohibitive. However, it is not uncommon for venue groups and larger hotel chains to take their own stand at international exhibitions, as they have multiple properties to showcase – and the marketing budgets to support this level of investment in exhibiting.

However at smaller, national or sub-national exhibitions, there can be a number of advantages of opting for the stand-alone alternative. The principal benefit is the boost that an individual stand, prominently decorated with the appropriate brand messages, can bring to the venue's profile in the market. Negotiations on the stand are also more discreet, in the absence of other, competing, exhibitors who may overhear such discussions between exhibitors and visitors.

Exhibiting at smaller shows can be more cost-effective, when the exhibition organiser opts for the use of a shell-scheme system. This 'egalitarian' approach to stand design and allocation means that each exhibitor hires the same, basic, shell-scheme stand of identical dimensions, giving each exhibitor a similar level of prominence at the show. While being less visually-striking overall, this system can create less of a drain on exhibitors' marketing budgets. Moreover, the benefits in terms of pre-show marketing and planning are the same regardless of the size of stand, which is another advantage. Occasionally, exhibitions opt to provide a mixture of systems. For example, the Square Meal Venues and Events exhibition in London has large stand spaces but also a good mix of smaller shell scheme spaces for exhibitors.

Clearly, a venue can opt for different alternatives out of the above three, according to the exhibition in question. For example, it is not uncommon for a venue to share a stand with other exhibitors at a major international exhibition, but to have its own, individual, stand for smaller national or regional shows.

Design of the stand

Of those venues in need of an individual stand, very few would even consider the possibility of designing and creating it by themselves. Even one aspect of that task – the health-and-safety regulations to be observed in the construction of the stand – would make the undertaking far too daunting for them to take on alone. In reality, most venues' marketing/ sales staff engage and work with a creative agency to design the stand, and the creative agency in turn works with a stand contractor to take care of logistical matters. These agencies are the experts in producing effective stands that can be used over and over again at different exhibitions.

Stand design has evolved greatly in past decades, as any glimpse at photographs of exhibitions from the 1970s and 1980s will confirm. Much more is known now about what makes stands effective in attracting visitors and making their visit to the stand enjoyable. The science of exhibition stand design and stand presentation suggests that:

☐   The graphics on the stand should be visually striking and strictly in line with the venue's brand. The wording and graphics should make it immediately clear to the visitor: that the exhibitor is a venue for meetings and events; where it is located; and what its key characteristics are (size, style of building, unique selling points). All of this, however, must be achieved with the minimum number of actual words – and judicious use of carefully-selected images.

☐   The design of the stand should be sufficiently flexible to enable it to be used year after year. One way of ensuring this is to make certain that the graphics can be changed in order to reflect any change in the messages to be transmitted by the stand's graphics at future exhibitions. A stand designed to be flexible also allows the structure to be adapted to fit differently sized space at various exhibitions.

☐   The stand should be visible from a distance and easily located.

6

Some exhibitions offer the possibility of stand-holders suspending a banner or inflated globe from the ceiling directly above their stand. When such devices are branded with the exhibiting venue's name and logo, it can make the stand much more prominent and therefore easier to find.

☐ The layout of the stand should be open and inviting, regardless of its size. There should be no form of barrier or obstruction (for example, a counter) that prevents visitors from walking on to the stand or discourages them from approaching the people working on it.

☐ Modern stand layout often includes a dedicated space where exhibitors can sit down and have a meeting or even negotiate with prospects, away from distractions and other visitors to the stand. In the case of the more elaborate 'double-decker' exhibition stands, this private space may be on the upper level.

☐ Putting material such as brochures, at the back of the stand encourages visitors to enter the stand space, giving venue staff the opportunity to engage with them. It also discourages material being consumed by 'brochure-eaters', that bizarre breed of exhibition visitors whose only apparent objective in attending is to amass as many brochures, pens and other give-aways as they can.

☐ Adding some kind of eye-catching 'attractor' to the stand can give the casual passer-by a reason to pause and spend time there – which in turn gives those working on the stand the opportunity to engage with them. It could be something as simple as a prize draw that visitors can enter by leaving their business cards in a bowl (these can be used to expand the venue's database). Movement of any kind tends to attract the attention of passers-by, and for that reason many venues have a video tour of their facility running on a loop on one or more screens on their stand. Humour can be another effective way of attracting attention to an exhibition stand. VisitSweden successfully experimented with the use of a comic magician whose entertaining shows regularly attracted crowds to their stand at EIBTM and IMEX. During the shows, the Swedish exhibitors 'worked the crowd' by distributing marketing material to, and collecting business cards from, the spectators.

The Methodist Central Hall in London memorably hired a 'looka-like' of Her Majesty the Queen to be present on their stand at an exhibition, generating large numbers of visitors keen to get close to the royal doppelganger!

Finally, the stand's location is another important factor in determining how many visitors it will receive at an exhibition. The flow of visitor traffic is different at each exhibition venue, and it largely depends on the floor plan. This is another factor that should be noted by any venue manager visiting an exhibition in order to decide whether or not to invest.

Some areas of the exhibition will naturally have more flow of traffic, but these locations usually come at a premium, while the more cost-effective spaces may be in a quieter part of the exhibition venue. It is also worth noting that some locations with a lot of footfall may also be very noisy – for example stands located next to a stage used for presentations or entertainment.

Before the exhibition

One of the major reasons for lack of success at any exhibition is insufficient forward planning on the part of the exhibitor. Those exhibitors who do little more than pay for stand-hire and turn up on day one of the exhibition run a high risk of being disappointed at the low level of interest in their presence at the show, most often manifested by insufficient numbers of visitors to their stand.

There are many actions that venue managers can take in order to avoid this situation and each one helps boost their return on investment from the exhibition. Advance communication is the key element in preparing to exhibit at any show, and it takes two forms, external communication and internal communication.

■ External communication

☐ Managers can – and should – take advantage of all the pre-show marketing opportunities offered by the exhibition organisers. These opportunities are always clearly listed in the material sent by the organisers to exhibitors at the time of booking stand space.

At the most basic level, each exhibitor is asked to forward their details (name of the venue, short description, contact details, etc.) to be included in the show catalogue. It is essential that exhibitors get this description absolutely right, as it is this description that drives many hosted buyers and other visitors to the stand. But most meetings industry exhibition organisers will offer exhibitors further marketing opportunities, such as the chance to send them news items about the venue, which they can include in their pre-show promotion or in the daily magazine published at the exhibition. These opportunities are invariably time-limited, therefore venue managers need to ensure that they meet all of the relevant deadlines set by the organisers, for sending them the material requested.

☐ Effective forward planning for attending an exhibition also involves venue managers using their own databases to contact their prospects and clients, informing them that the venue will be exhibiting at the show and (crucially) that *they will be announcing something new* there. (It may even be possible for the venue manager to do a targeted email-shot using the database of visitors created by the exhibition organisers – although they will usually have to pay for this service). Clients and prospects are much more likely to visit a venue's stand if they have been told in advance that by doing so they will find out something new about the venue – a refurbishment, expansion of the facility, or simply some exciting plans for the future. It is the marketing manager's role to determine which message or story will be most effective in generating interest and visitation to the stand. For new venues, the question of which message to transmit is entirely straightforward, as the opening of the venue itself is the scoop.

☐ For contacting large numbers of prospects and clients, an email-shot is the most obvious technique. However, it is worth bearing in mind that these recipients will most likely also be receiving similar messages from other, competing venues in the weeks leading up to the exhibition. One way of distinguishing the message from all of the others is to personalise it in the 'subject' line, with the recipient's name. This may lower its chances of simply being deleted unread. In the case of VIP prospects and clients, an even more personal approach is for the venue staff to telephone them individually, with the invitation to visit the stand during the exhibition.

☐ The invitation to call at the venue's stand may either be open – to drop in at any time; or it may be to attend a special event at a specific time, for example a drinks reception. Venue managers may even decide to organise a special evening event for key prospects/clients visiting the exhibition, such as a select dinner in a restaurant. Such initiatives are an important aspect of key account management and developing a relationship with clients and potential clients.

☐ Venues may also choose to promote their presence at a forthcoming exhibition by advertising in the meetings industry press by paying for an advertisement in the magazine or magazines read by their prospects. On the one hand, this method has the advantage of reaching a large number of readers – and the venue can make the advertisement visually attractive through an effective use of images and graphics; but on the other it is something of a scattershot approach that lacks the individual touch that a personalised message can bring.

■ Internal communication

Internal communication is also vital, and this can take two main forms: (1) pre-exhibition training and briefing, and (2) on-site reviews during the exhibition.

Pre-exhibition training

This is particularly relevant for new members of the venue's staff or those working on an exhibition stand for the first time. This can take the form of a simple list of exhibition 'Do's and Do nots' to guide inexperienced exhibitors in how they can be most effective while working on the venue's stand. These are likely to include the examples of advice given in Figure 6.2.

DO

- Look fresh and well-presented.

- Wear something that makes it clear that you are working on the stand: e.g. a polo-shirt bearing the venue's logo.

- Come out of the stand to attract visitors' attention.

- Be personable and welcome each visitor with a smile, eye contact and a good solid handshake.

- Acknowledge each visitor who walks on to the stand, even if you are in discussion with another visitor.

- Ask questions – propose solutions.

DO NOT

- Leave the stand unattended.

- Stay anchored to the stand. Walk around from time to time to see what competing venues are doing on their stands.

- Over-indulge in the parties and receptions that are held around exhibitions.

- Eat or drink on the stand, except during receptions hosted by the venue.

- Run out of brochures or business cards.

- Arrive after the exhibition has begun or leave before it has ended.

Figure 6.2: Exhibitor guidelines

Staff working at an exhibition for the first time may need guidance on how to engage with visitors. While giving them a pre-determined 'script' to follow is generally inadvisable, some basic guidelines can make inexperienced staff more effective in this role. At the very least, they should be advised to avoid the stock phrase 'Do you book events?' This sounds amateurish and uninspired. Rather, staff should be encouraged to engage in a more natural-sounding conversation with visitors: 'How are you?', 'Are you having a good day?' before asking something along the lines of 'Do you know about our venue?' Conversations that are natural and friendly, warm and welcoming, without sounding fake or rehearsed increase the probability that visitors will engage with exhibitors on their stand.

The pre-exhibition briefing also takes the form of informing all members of the venue staff working on the exhibition stand of the message or messages to be transmitted and the objectives of exhibiting at the show. Objectives might include: a branding exercise (increasing the venue's visibility in the market), making new contacts, identifying people to be invited into the venue for site inspections, expanding (or, in the case of new venues, creating) a database of prospects, and generating new enquiries.

Before the trade show, the venue manager should inform all exhibiting staff of some key, measurable outcomes from exhibiting that will be used to calculate the return on investment. These targets should be discussed and agreed upon, rather than imposed, so that all members of the exhibiting team subscribe to them.

Examples of measurable outcomes from exhibiting may include:

☐ The number of new leads found, to simply build the venue's database.

☐ The number of 'warm' leads generated, where 'warm' can be defined as leads with immediate or imminent potential, and who will be quickly followed up by venue sales staff.

☐ The number of enquires received (these can be broken down further into associations/agents/corporates/industry segments, according to the venue's overall business plan.

☐ The value of enquiries received.

☐ The number of sales appointments made or site inspections/famtrips booked.

☐ The value of business confirmed. This may not be realised until a date long after the exhibition, but it can only be tracked if each enquiry is recorded as being a lead from a particular exhibition.

At the exhibition

■   Communication between venue staff members

Internal communication in the form of on-site review sessions during the exhibition involves daily follow-up and daily stand briefings at the show, in order to review the venue staff's performance as a whole and to evaluate the extent to which they are reaching the objectives that were set. Such sessions may be held each morning before visitors arrive at the exhibition, but there is much to be said for them taking place immediately after the show closes each day, while the team's performance is still fresh in everyone's mind. They provide an opportunity to identify any problems and to discuss any changes of tactics necessary to take into account unforeseen developments at the exhibition.

■   Qualifying visitors and recording actions to be taken

At exhibitions, it is vital that venue staff are able to qualify or categorise visitors to the stand and to accurately record the actions to be taken regarding each visitor. In this respect, exhibitors are engaged in turning visitors to their stand into actual leads and preparing for the work that they will do after the show has closed and they return to their place of work. Judicious questioning of visitors to the stand will help determine what stage they are at, regarding both their degree of familiarity with the venue and their planning of forthcoming events.

Technology can help simplify this task and save valuable time at the exhibition. Visitors' badges almost always display a barcode which identifies them on an individual basis by linking them with the personal information that they submitted when registering to attend the exhibition. This information, which can be accessed by exhibitors, includes many of the basic facts that venues need to know about their prospects: their name, company, contact details, the size and types of events they organise, budgets, the destinations they typically use for their events, and so on.

Many venues further classify visitors to their stand by creating, on a sheet of card or paper, their own list of visitor categories and actions to be taken, each represented by a different barcode. Examples of visitor categories could be: 'Interested in space for large association conferences', 'Interested in space for regular board meetings', 'Interested in space for product launches', 'Time-waster', etc.; and examples of actions to be taken could include: 'Invite for a site inspection', 'Send DVD of venue', and 'Add to press contacts list'. By scanning each visitor's badge and then the barcodes representing the appropriate visitor category and action or actions to be taken, precious time can be saved for the all-important process of getting to know the visitor and their needs and matching those needs with what the venue can offer.

It is vital for all venue staff working on the stand to remember that what matters in terms of the leads generated from any exhibition is the quality of those leads, not the quantity. It is their quality that will ultimately determine how many leads eventually become clients of the venue, as a result of meeting at an exhibition.

■ Networking opportunities

Most exhibitions include a social programme, in the form of evening receptions, cocktails and parties that provide exhibitors and visitors opportunities to meet each other and network on a more informal basis. All members of the venue staff exhibiting at the show should be encouraged to attend these events, equipped with an ample supply of business cards, and to network widely with exhibition visitors. Evening events are not the time or place for 'hard-selling' activities or negotiations, but they can be a very useful source of new leads; and buyers encountered at evening events can be invited to visit the venue's stand the following day, to continue any discussions initiated at the social event.

Inexperienced exhibitors occasionally forget that during this social element of exhibitions they are still on duty and regarded by others as representing their venue, even in the relaxed, informal atmosphere of networking sessions and parties. Alcohol flows freely at these events and can have an immediate and powerful effect on exhibitors who may be feeling exhausted after a day of standing up and hungry as a result of being too busy on their stand to take a lunch break. In addition, younger members of staff may be tempted to remain at evening social events until the very end – by which time an 'evening' event has become a 'morning event'. The lack of valuable sleeping hours that this entails means that irrepressible party animals rarely look their best or perform at optimum levels on the exhibition stand the following day.

6

The exhibiting team needs to be reminded of these pitfalls and of their ongoing responsibility towards the reputation and brand of the venue. Moderation and professionalism are the keys to enjoying and making the most of the exhibition's social programme.

Venues with the good fortune to be located in the actual city where the exhibition is taking place have the opportunity to create their own evening or pre-/post-exhibition events for buyers attending the show. Selected buyers can be entertained by venues at such social events that may be combined with a tour of the venue itself. The local convention bureau may be able to assist with the selection of buyers and the logistics of the event.

But even when the exhibition is not held in the city where the venue is located, there may be potential benefits to venues if their local convention bureau organises 'add-on' events for hosted buyers. For example, London & Partners, the convention bureau of the UK capital, regularly invites US-based hosted buyers to IMEX in Frankfurt, but also brings them to London after the exhibition, specifically to look at London venues. This adds value to the hosted buyers' transatlantic trip and provides London venues with a further opportunity to engage with American prospects.

■ Educational opportunities

Almost all exhibitions include a daily seminar programme of presentations from experts, researchers and practitioners, covering topics such as trends in the market and advice on effective techniques relevant to professional practice in the meetings industry. These presentations, usually taking place in seminar rooms separate from the exhibition floor, are open to exhibitors and well as visitors and represent a valuable source of education for venue staff – on condition that they can leave the stand without it being under-staffed. From time to time, exhibitors have been known to complain that seminar programmes of this type are counter-productive as they temporarily remove some buyers from the exhibition floor, thereby reducing the number of potential visitors to the stands. However, it is certainly the case that for many visitors the seminar programme may be the main reason they are at the exhibition in the first place. Therefore the educational element of most exhibitions helps boost the number of visitors. A more justified criticism of educational seminars, perhaps, is that when they take place on the exhibition floor the noise they generate can be a source of nuisance and distraction for those working on, or visiting, nearby stands.

After the exhibition

Many experienced venue managers would argue that the most important work related to exhibiting takes place after the show has closed and exhibitors have gone back to their offices. That is when venue managers should begin maximising the sales and marketing opportunities arising from the contacts made at the exhibition. Exhibitors who fail to make adequate use of the contacts they have made at the show are missing the most valuable of opportunities to boost their return on investment.

The time that exhibitors have to spend with each visitor to their stand is rarely sufficient, due to the fact that buyers' time is generally limited – now more than ever – and therefore some form of follow-up is vital. For example, it may be that, for prospects on a tight schedule at the exhibition, the venue manager has to agree that he or she will call them to arrange an appointment or site inspection upon returning to the office.

Follow-up should be undertaken on a personal note, for example through the use of a personalised email, reminding the recipient of where the initial meeting took place, and providing the material requested. Most venue managers make this form of follow-up an urgent priority upon their return to their place of work. But an argument can be made for waiting a week or so before sending material, in order to avoid it being simply lost among all of the other mass of material that is sent to visitors immediately after any exhibition. In any case, it is advisable to agree in advance with the recipient when material will be sent to them.

However, in the case of an exhibiting venue receiving a specific enquiry from a visitor to the stand – the visitor has a specific event for which they are actively seeking a venue – much more immediate action is necessary on the part of the venue staff. They should without delay call colleagues back in the office to check availability and prepare a proposal for the prospect's event. Winning events in this way is not unknown at exhibitions, and from the perspective of the venue securing

6

even one piece of business in this way can make the exhibition entirely worthwhile in terms of return on investment.

On a more strategic level, it is vital that venues monitor the longer-term value of the contacts made at any exhibition, as this will guide future management decisions on whether to exhibit at the same show again. 'Has it been worth it?' is a question notoriously difficult to answer when attempting to judge the return on investment from exhibiting at any meetings industry show, especially if an attempt is made to base that judgment on short-term benefits accruing from a one-off experience of exhibiting. Many venues with extensive experience of exhibiting at meetings industry shows can cite examples of events that they have won, based on encounters with buyers at exhibitions held many years previously. In addition to the more tangible benefits of meetings and events booked at the venue as a direct result of exhibiting, it is important for venues to take into account the many intangible, but no less real, advantages of the many networking and educational opportunities that exhibitions offer. A more reasonable question for venues, when considering the benefits from exhibiting, may be 'What can we do to increase our return on investment from exhibitions?' This chapter has indicated the many ways in which venues can maximise the benefits that meetings industry shows, large and small, offer their exhibitors.

Hotel Granvia Kyoto's success through trade shows

A hotel venue shares the valuable lessons it has learned from participating in meetings industry exhibitions.

Background

In Kyoto, Japan, there are four hotels capable of hosting major business events, including two global brands with a global sales presence (Westin and Hyatt). Granvia is a national brand but Hotel Granvia Kyoto sees the potential of the global MICE market in a changing business environment in which one of Japan's traditional source markets, weddings, is beginning to evolve (weddings are getting smaller and moving out of hotels) and shrink (Japan's population peaked in the early 2000s and continued decline is projected).

Hotel Granvia Kyoto. Photo: Wikipedia Commons

History of our involvement in trade shows

Hotel Granvia Kyoto's experience of using trade shows consisted largely of experimentation in exhibiting at different exhibitions for the meetings market, beginning with those in North America such as PRIME and IT&ME. We also experimented with different levels of participation - simply exhibiting; sponsoring a lunch at the exhibition; and sponsoring events within the trade show.

Reviewing the return on investment from participation in trade shows, we have focussed on exhibiting at IMEX and at AIME since 2008.

Our hotel management has noted that our local competitors in Kyoto, Westin and Hyatt, appear to be less active at meetings industry trade shows, relying instead on their centralised global marketing teams to be present.

The turning point

Our first trade show breakthrough came in 2007 when Kanako Murayama, our Director of Overseas Marketing at the time, met Phoebe Boelter, the organiser of the annual conference of FIRST, an international confederation of trusted computer incident response teams who cooperatively handle computer security incidents and promote incident prevention programmes (http://www.first.org/events/agm/2009),

6

at IT&ME in Chicago. Their meeting at IT&ME resulted in Granvia winning the FIRST conference, beating not only global competitors in the city and in other regions of Japan (Okinawa was also under consideration) but also, more importantly, competitors based in other countries in the region – Singapore, Malaysia and other Asian destinations were also under consideration for the conference. The post trade show follow-up and hard work on behalf of the hotel management paid off when the contract for the 375-delegate conference was signed by the organisers.

This was the first significant direct contact with overseas meeting planners for our hotel and it set the benchmark for the measurement of our future successes.

Lessons we have learnt - target markets

An effective choice of trade show means careful consideration of what the venue's target markets are. As a relatively premium-priced property, we recognised that North American, European and the relatively short-haul Australian MICE markets were viable targets. So we were most successful when we exhibited at trade shows attracting buyers from those regions. We also came to understand the value of exhibiting at trade shows specifically aimed at the meetings market, as this fitted in well with the clear distinction that we ourselves make between our marketing strategy for MICE buyers and our strategy for other source markets, such as leisure travel.

Lessons we have learnt - making most of the time spent onsite

The trade show is the one opportunity in any given year to introduce your product and your staff to an entire industry, an opportunity from which every bit of value must be squeezed.

At a mere 155cm in height, our marketing manager Yuka Murata could be easy overlooked in the busy environment of a trade show. So, to stand out in the crowd, she brings a little taste of Kyoto tradition, hospitality and fun to every trade show she attends, by wearing a brightly coloured kimono. She uses the attention that she attracts as she walks around the exhibition as an opportunity to share a smile, exchange a business card, and make another new connection.

We believe that trade shows are not just a place to disseminate information about the property; most importantly they are a place to gather information about the direction the industry is going in and also to find out how to serve individual clients. In addition, when an industry gathers together in vast numbers for a few days, networking opportunities abound, and Granvia staff members actively take part in events taking place on the fringe of trade shows, such as parties and conference dinners.

Lessons we have learnt - staffing trade shows

As with any aspect of business management, allocation of the proper resources in the right place is paramount. Hotel Granvia Kyoto makes a point of sending the right staff to trade shows. For example, the aforementioned Yuka Murata with her natural personality, curiosity, persistence, and sweet and attractive manner is ideally suited to the role of representing our hotel at trade shows. She is certainly the key to our getting the right connections at trade shows and the reason why every trade show we attend wins us business that more than pays for the participation costs

6

Lessons we have learnt - the importance of a partnership approach to trade shows

At the Hotel Granvia Kyoto, we understand that in order to win business for the hotel and venue, we must first of all sell our destination, Kyoto. To achieve this, we operate in partnership at trade shows, with the Kyoto Convention Bureau and other local suppliers such as kimono providers, the Kyoto Cycling Tour Project, as well as with Destination Management Companies and even other hotels when necessary. Each partner has enough knowledge of all the other partners to be able to promote their services and their facilities to visitors at the trade show just as well as they promote their own.

The relationship with Kyoto Convention Bureau means that, after trade shows we have both attended, we can work together to follow up planner leads and requests, liaise on behalf of clients with other Kyoto suppliers, and provide support to KCB familiarisation trips that result from connections made at those trade shows.

In recognition of the importance of demonstrating strong partner relationships, we actively co-exhibit at some trade shows with a destination management company, The J Team. The close collaboration of a DMC and our hotel makes an attractive combination for meeting planners considering Kyoto as a destination for their events. Looking at the city from the client's perspective in this way wins us new insights into their requirements and, ultimately, new business

We are not selling/promoting hotel accommodation and function space. We are selling a Kyoto experience that the planner is looking for. We never forget that our hotel means nothing without the great city fabric that is Kyoto, its culture, architecture and people. From that premise, we also use trade shows to remind buyers that we believe that the joint priority of both planner and venue is to provide the highest quality experience for events participants.

Online sources of further information

International Congress and Convention Association (ICCA): Guide to meetings
industry exhibitions

http://www.iccaworld.com/evps/evresults.cfm?classid=2

UFI (The Global Association of the Exhibition Industry) Successful Exhibit
Marketing by Bob Dallmeyer

http://www.ufi.org/Public/Default.aspx?Clef_SITESMAPS=157

Step-by-Step Exhibiting Guide.

http://www.trade-show-guide.com/articles/exhibitingguide.html

The Green Guide to Exhibiting.

http://www.marketingdonut.co.uk/marketing/exhibitions-and-events/
exhibiting/the-green-guide-to-exhibiting

Skyline Trade Show Tips

www.skylinetradeshowtips.com/100-trade-show-lead-generation-ideas/

6

7 The Changing Market Environment

The market environment within which the meetings industry operates is in a constant state of flux, being endlessly re-shaped by economic, social, technological and demographic factors far beyond the control of the professionals working in meetings venues.

In order to survive and thrive, venues must rise to the ongoing challenges associated with satisfying ever more sophisticated and diverse needs within this market environment. This chapter examines some of the key factors currently affecting supply and demand in the meetings market, and explores how meetings facilities may adapt in order to continue winning business and adding value to their clients' events.

Advances in venue design

One of the most significant changes facing venues in the 21st century is the transformation in the ways in which meetings are being planned and designed. Traditional meetings models are being challenged by the rise of innovative alternatives, and as the design and demands of meetings evolve, so must the venues that host them.

In *The Future of the Meetings Industry* report published by the National Conference Centre, the author notes that with the vast amount of content available online and the ability to watch a speaker present virtually, the need for participants to travel and attend a conference in order to get access to information has changed radically. Moreover, in times of economic uncertainty, attendees become more selective about the conferences they choose to attend. As a result, a growing number of innovative conference designers have reformatted the traditional conference design by creating participant-driven events with greater and more effective opportunities for networking, and a variety of settings to facilitate collaboration among attendees.

According to the report, participant-driven events are fundamentally different to the traditional conference model, largely composed of sessions with seats facing the front of the room and speakers providing a 'lesson' for attendees. Until recently, for the most part, the meetings industry considered successful conferences to consist of a keynote speaker and pre-planned material presented to the attendees from start to finish – essentially a passive learning experience for attendees. But now, when anyone can watch the keynote speaker on YouTube, conference content is increasingly not what the organisers think the attendees want to learn, but rather a general consensus from the attendees on what they want to gain from the experience. Today's attendees are more willing to attend a conference with active learning, based on principles of adult learning, that fits their needs, fosters collaboration and addresses concepts they are most interested in discovering.

Adrian Segar, a conference designer by trade and the author of *Conferences That Work: Creating Events That People Love*, explains how adults learn most effectively: 'Most adults are capable of finding out what they need [in a conference] rather than someone else determining what they need. Attendees have the capability of directing their learning'. He places significant emphasis on the 70-20-10 rule, which maintains that adults learn 70% of their job from peers (known as social learning), with another 20% learned by reading or, increasingly, internet research (self-directed learning) and only 10% from formal learning such as training. He strongly believes that the future of meetings will continue to occur in venues such as conference centres. However, rather than a traditional classroom setting, the focus will be on space that promotes social learning and allows for informal learning groups so that attendees can learn from one another, as well as from speakers.

In the research conducted by the National Conference Centre into how conference innovators are changing the future of the meetings industry, one common theme resonates throughout – the emphasis on helping people connect and interact with each other at conferences. Tom Condon, who specialises in designing meeting experiences for Steelcase, the world's largest office environments manufacturer is quoted in *The Future of the Meetings Industry* report as saying: 'People want to connect to speakers or other colleagues at a conference. Conference organisers are listening and reacting by creating more opportunities for engagement'. As examples of how this can be achieved, he notes that conference innovators are creating longer lunch breaks, building space where individuals can meet on a casual basis, and designated lounge areas with time-slots for attendees to have conversations with presenters – all of which promote quality face time and one-on-one interaction.

Condon's recent work with Steelcase has focused on building a variety of different settings for attendees. At conferences such as Technology Entertainment and Design (TED) in 2011, Steelcase developed a variety of settings that they refer to as 'a palette of places'. This environment was created by dividing the venue's ballroom into different zones such as an area with bean bag chairs, a large section of café tables at the back of the room with media space for attendees who chose to blog, quiet zones with lounge chairs and table tops to take notes or accomplish work. Condon describes this form of layout as exciting and energetic, "(For attendees) it helps foster the idea that this conference is unique, enjoyable and this space is going to help me connect to other people."

The *Maritz Future of Meetings Survey* also highlighted meeting planners' interest in venues responding to changing conference formats by providing informal gathering spaces for attendees. Respondents' 'wish-list' included such items such as:

☐   'Provide more casual quiet spaces for less formal interaction than meeting rooms. Places where people can "do stuff" as they talk and meet, as they do in their own homes.'

☐   'Flexible networking space, lots of space that meets the needs of different groups, events, people, etc. Lots of lounge sofa-type seating with wireless to allow people to network and stay connected.'

It is clear that as future meetings become less structured and provide more free-time for participants to network, this will require that there be well-designed, comfortable, separate spaces and hospitality services available throughout a meeting. The old breakout rooms and fixed times for coffee breaks will be replaced by a looser structure that allows for constant interaction throughout the course of an event. Ideally, these new spaces will also be available to participants outside of the formal meeting schedule. Of course they will also have to boast all the technical and communication requirements the participants will want (e.g., power outlets, connectivity, etc.).

The wish for flexibility in venue design resonates throughout the *Maritz Future of Meetings Survey*. Jim Ruszala, senior director of marketing at Maritz Travel, defines a flexible venue as "having plenty of room for general and breakout sessions. Also, going beyond traditional room settings; for instance, creating more of an informal room set-up that is more attendee-friendly and engaging. It's more about creating good, lasting experiences". Other respondents commented on the need for flexibility:

☐   'Facilities will need to be looking at how they design space and how flexible that space can become'

☐   'Make especially the large meeting rooms multifunctional and flexible'

☐   'The venue of the future will be smaller, highly technical – to be able to offer the combo Face-to-Face and Face-to-Screen meetings.'

At the most ambitious end of the spectrum, survey respondents and sector experts predict these informal gathering spaces will be available to meeting participants twenty-four hours a day and provide all-day access to food and beverage, as suggested by these proposals:

☐   '…have more and more appropriate seating outside meeting rooms for gathering. Encourage informal gathering by having places with food open 24 hours a day. People at meetings/in venues are on different time zones and may want a place to gather and meet others.'

☐   'Food and beverage kiosks that offer regular and healthy alternatives — 24 hours a day.'

Venues already offering any of these features that can satisfy the demands of evolving meetings formats should ensure that they are given due prominence in marketing materials, site inspections and any negotiations with clients.

Updating hotel meeting facilities

(Based on an article by Jeanne O'Brien Coffey which appeared in the October 2010 edition of *Executive Travel* magazine)

When the Washington Hilton welcomed its first meeting, Lyndon B. Johnson was President, banks of payphones lined public spaces and smoking at work was widely accepted. The 11-storied property opened in 1965 and quickly became synonymous with some of the most prestigious meetings in the capital. It has hosted the official Presidential Inaugural Ball every four years since 1969, the Washington Correspondents Dinner for the past 30 years and countless politicians and celebrities.

While payphones have all but disappeared (and smoking is severely restricted), the property's meeting space had fallen behind the times, lacking the connectivity and flexibility that planners increasingly demand. The property's largest meeting space, the Exhibit Hall, consisted of 45,000 square feet of indivisible space, filled with columns. It was used for a variety of large events but well suited for none of them.

"You can have a lot of space but no flexibility," says Bob Donovan, vice president of meetings and travel services at the American Hospital Association. The AHA has been holding its annual membership meeting at the Washington Hilton for close to 40 years; in that time, the event has grown into a 1,800-person gathering of high-level hospital administrators, CEOs and trustees, along with the staff of state hospital associations.

7

"Meetings have changed a lot, and for a meeting like this, you keep adding meetings to it and adding meetings to it," Donovan notes. In addition to the main gathering, 35 or 40 states want to hold caucuses, as well as executive sessions and training sessions. "It's a lot of moving pieces and a lot of breakout space."

Time for a change

Renovations at the Washington Hilton have taken place incrementally over the years, as meeting space has been updated here and the guestrooms there. When the property changed hands in 2007, the new owners realized a wholesale restoration was in order—to the tune of $149 million. The hotel and its meeting areas had become an amalgam of trends from different decades, and its lack of flexible space meant it was losing out on significant portions of today's meeting market.

"Our customers told us we need more space, we need more flexible space, we need more breakout space, we need more divisibility and more flexibility," says Frank Passante, mid-Atlantic regional director of sales and marketing at Hilton Hotels. The total meeting space available at the hotel remains unchanged, at 110,000 square feet—but it is more purpose-built and adjustable. For example, the new Columbia Hall, which will replace the Exhibit Hall, can be used in one piece or divided into as many as 12 rooms.

The two-year process left not one square foot of the meeting space untouched, including a new colour palette and improvements in back-of-the-house systems and connectivity. But the crown jewel of the project is a new self-contained conference centre geared specifically to small-to-midsize top-level meetings—a hot trend today. "There is tremendous demand for those small-to-midsize meetings: training meetings, high-level board meetings, advisory meetings," Passante says. "But we did not have the ability to offer it prior to adding the Heights Executive Conference Centre."

The space was purpose-built not only for this size confab, but also to ensure that attendees get the most out of every meeting. "To justify face-to-face meetings, customers today demand productivity." Passante says. "They are measuring ROI and are trying to make their meetings as productive and efficient as possible. We believe productive meetings happen best in purpose-built space."

To that end, the new centre, which replaced a wing of ground floor guestrooms, consists of nine rooms geared specifically for all-day learning. Hardtop tables with easy laptop connections and ergonomic chairs have replaced banquet chairs and tables with linens, and floor-to-ceiling windows flood the rooms with natural light (with blackout shades available for presentations, of course). Passante says that the new space works for planners on several levels. "There's really nothing like this in Washington. This is not just terrific meeting space, this is a distraction-free learning environment completely away from the rest of the hotel."

Technology updating

Not surprisingly, technology plays a huge role in the new conference center and throughout all the redesigned space, from Wi-Fi in the meeting rooms to recessed electronic projection screens. Each room also has a ceiling-mounted projector "periscope" containing the projector mount, power and data outlet. When needed, it slides down from the ceiling; when not in use, it slides up, leaving just a white disk on the ceiling and hiding all the infrastructure above.

"If the expression [was] 'Time is money,' it might be changed to 'Connectivity is money' as we move forward," says Ryan Langlois, an associate at Washington, D.C.–based architecture and design firm OPX, which handled the renovation. He adds that just providing connectivity isn't enough. "You still need power outlets to drive all these devices, and today's business traveller is not shy about seeking them out."

To that end, the Heights Center, as well as the Terrace and Concourse meeting spaces, offer laptop touchdown spots—standing-height ledges with power outlets above the counter—in the pre-function space. These spots also serve another meeting space design trend: maximizing opportunities for networking.

"Realizing that business and connections happen at multiple points during a meeting, the design provides for locations to help guests engage with one another at multiple levels," Langlois says, adding that the computer touchdown stations provide a natural gathering spot. Even the hallways include new seating areas designed to enable more social interactions between meetings, he adds. In the middle of the meeting centre, a communal breakout area for food service can serve as a nexus of activity for both the meeting spaces and as a new outdoor terrace.

The centre is the ideal setting for executive sessions, says AHA's Donovan, whose group was among the first to use the facilities, along with almost all of the Washington Hilton's 110,000 square feet of meeting space. The full renovation wasn't scheduled for completion until about a month after the AHA's annual meeting, but attendees got a taste of things to come, and Donovan liked what he saw.

In fact, the AHA was so excited by the prospects of the completed space that it included "Come back next year—it'll be a whole new show" in the meeting script.

7

Donovan says he is returning to the property in a few months to assess changes to his meeting's flow for next year, and he sees new energy in the reconfigured space. "I'm sure we'll make some interesting decisions on how we can move things around next year."

Donovan is also anxiously awaiting the brand-new Columbia Hall. The 30,000-square-foot, column-free space will host several AHA sessions, eliminating a number of quick turnarounds in the existing space. The event's 800-person awards luncheon, previously held in the Exhibit Hall, will take place in the new hall as well.

"[Previously], we had to put in 20 TVs—one on every post—so people could see the speaker," says Donovan, adding that the event, which has attracted such speakers as surgeon general Regina Benjamin and former secretary of state Colin Powell, will be a much better fit in the new hall.

"We can't wait to go back," he adds. "I think with the changes they've made, we'll be partners for a long time to come."

Advances in technology

Advances in technology provide both challenges as well as opportunities for the meetings industry. On the one hand, products such as videoconferencing and Telepresence provide compelling alternatives to face to face, delivering cost savings and sustainability benefits. But a recent study conducted by Christine Duffy and Mary Beth McEuan for Cornell University School of Hotel Administration's Center for Hospitality Research found that face-to-face meetings, and not the newest virtual meeting technologies, are the most advantageous means for successfully achieving most business outcomes. They concluded that face-to-face meetings were consistently more effective in:

1 capturing participants' attention

2 inspiring a positive emotional climate and catalysing collaboration, and

3 building human networks and relationships.

Nevertheless, it is undeniable that technology is now a permanent part of the meetings mix, not least by adding value to face-to-face events, for example via online delegate registration and participants' use of mobile devices and social media during meetings. Two contemporary trends have particular bearing on the management and marketing of meetings venues: the demand for growing connectivity for events; and the use of the social media for venue marketing purposes.

Connectivity

It is widely agreed that the increased reliance on technology to help facilitate meetings will create new demands for meeting venues, notably in the area of investment in technology. Crucially, meeting venues are increasingly finding that they need to provide ever greater levels of connectivity in order to attract meetings. For years, event organisers have selected sites based on rates, space and availability for desired dates. Now, many believe that it is necessary to add a fourth site selection consideration to the list: bandwidth capability.

Typical of 21st century meeting planners are the respondents in the *Maritz Future of Meetings Survey* research, who frequently mentioned the need for 'free Wi-Fi' and 'consistent Wi-Fi' at venues. Their comments also included the need for reliable mobile phone connectivity and having sufficient bandwidth to accommodate large numbers of devices. Similarly, in the Convention Industry Council and Hospitality Sales and Marketing Association International's publication, *Getting up to Speed: Event Bandwidth*, the authors emphasise that 'bandwidth configuration has become just as important to achieving an event's goals and objectives as compelling content, well presented and tasty food, adequate meeting space, and comfortable guest rooms'.

Shortcomings in these services can have a damaging impact on even technologically sophisticated venues. In 2010, the *New York Times* reported that Steve Jobs of Apple had to ask attendees to turn off their laptops and phones after his launching of the iPhone 4 was derailed because of an overloaded Wi-Fi network at the venue for the product launch.

While not all incidents caused by overloaded W-Fi networks are as dramatic as this, increasingly, participants complain to event planners and venue managers when the Internet access fails to meet their needs and expectations. As a result, unsatisfactory Internet experiences can cause groups to avoid rebooking venues where they have had a bad experience. Today Internet connectivity affects the entire meetings industry. Many of today's array of personal mobile devices such as tablet computers were not around three years ago. But consumers have adopted these new tools into their personal lives and work at an amazing pace, and they can bring with them as many as two or three data-hungry devices to events. The movement towards webcasting, streaming video, remote presentations, conference apps, social media, gamification and more to the event scene has rapidly created a huge and expanding demand for bandwidth.

But the report *Getting up to Speed: Event Bandwidth* notes that there is at present no fluency in bandwidth terminology to match the more familiar vocabulary used to describe, for example, room setups: 'Everyone understands what is meant by cabaret, theatre, and classroom style, for example. But familiarity with technology terminology is more limited. Starting the bandwidth conversation can be a challenge for both event planners and their hotel or other venue partners. Most people plead low or minimal technical knowledge'.

The report goes on to suggest that, at the very least, now is the time to start that conversation, with venue representatives taking steps to:

☐ Ask the customer the question, "Do you know the bandwidth and wireless device requirements for your group?"

☐ Ask about the group's past experiences. Have they had service or capacity issues?

☐ Know what the property's network service provider is capable of. Can it offer dedicated bandwidth for individual groups? What is the pricing for dedicated bandwidth? How many wireless devices can the network support?

☐ Know the bandwidth in the property's meeting facilities, sleeping rooms, public space and food outlets. At what point do those max out?

☐ Know who at the property can provide more information, additional guidance and technical expertise, whether that is an in-house expert or someone who manages the venue's relationship with the network service provider.

But, regardless of the answers to the above questions, that fact remains that providing adequate bandwidth is an ongoing investment need for venues that host events, and it requires frequent updates in infrastructure at a minimum of every five years. Venues are generally run as businesses, and are therefore looking to achieve adequate returns on their investments. Meeting rapidly increasing demands for satisfactory Internet connectivity at events is expensive and like everything else that goes into a successful event, it costs somebody. This raises the all-important question of how long it will take meetings planners to realise that there is no such thing as 'free Wi-Fi'.

2012 Venue Trend Survey

Free WIFI

Do you offer free WIFI at your center?

151 venues answered

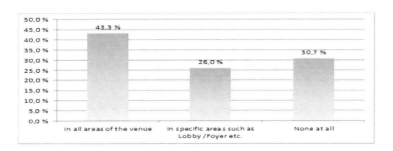

151 venues answered

International Congress and Convention Association

Twitter: #ICCA12

Figure 7.1: Availability of free WiFi, as reported to the 2012 Venue Trend Survey. Source Dobler-Jerabek (2012)

■   Social media

Web 2.0 applications, and in particular the social media are increasingly being used by businesses of all kinds as marketing tools, and venues are no exception. In a survey of ten of the UK's largest conference centres, published by Davidson in 2011, their use of the social media for marketing purposes, was found to be already significant and set to grow even more in the near future. Linkedin and Twitter were found to be the most popular applications, already used by six venues out of the ten surveyed, with other venues expressing their intention to adopt them into their marketing strategies before very long. Facebook was in use by five venues, followed by YouTube, used by three. One year later, in the *ICCA 2012 Venue Trends Survey*, in response to the question 'Does your venue use social media?' 80% of the 154 venues surveyed replied in the affirmative. However, only 47% of those using the social media monitored the actual success of these tools.

Social Media

If not, why?

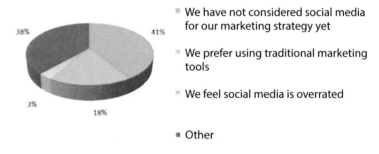

34 venues answered

Figure 7.2: Why venues are not using social media for marketing, as reported to the 2012 Venue Trend Survey. Source Dobler-Jerabek (2012)

Lack of effective monitoring of return on investment in time spent using the social media for venue marketing was also an issue highlighted by the findings of Davidson's survey in 2011. This may change as tools specifically created to enable the quantifying of return on investment in Web 2.0 tools become increasingly available. However, any misgivings about using the social media for this purpose were outweighed by the positive comments from venue sales and marketing staff and their advice to late adopters:

☐   We have used Twitter to join conversations that are already happening on the web – our opinion was that whether we decided to participate or not, people were talking about us already, and it would be foolish not to acknowledge it [. . .]. We went as far as to host a 'tweet-up' event, bringing together local businesses to talk about emerging web technologies. We even receive enquiries via Twitter.

☐ Always use it on a business level. I don't retweet anything particularly 'political'. Only tweet or retweet if it is useful or engaging to your followers. We have really raised our profile by working together through social media. It's a great success and keeps getting better!

☐ Monitor what is happening on YouTube with your venue – you do not know who is posting what.

☐ LinkedIn is a great form of media to promote. Join in discussions, make comments and help others. This will deliver great ROI.

☐ Individual members in the sales team use LinkedIn as a marketing tool on an individual basis, giving it a more personal feel.

☐ On a commercial level, we have picked up new business through enquiries from Twitter.

☐ Through the blogs going out through Twitter, we are reaching out to a really interesting audience.

☐ I use LinkedIn as a personal/business social media platform. I have really been able to raise my business profile through it. This was the first social media site I used and it's been incredible to develop connections for business.

In 2012, the International Association of Conference Centres published an extremely useful guide to using Web 2.0 applications in venue marketing, entitled *A Guide to Social Media*. The guide provides practical advice for venues on how they can successfully make use of Blogs, Twitter, Facebook Business Page, YouTube, LinkedIn, Flickr, Google+, Pinterest and other applications, with specific tips on how to make the most of them for venue sales and marketing. Initiatives of IACC members already making effective use of each application are highlighted as examples of good practice.

For example, in terms of how venues can use blogs to their advantage, the guide recommends:

1 Blog only if you have something to say! A blog isn't a soapbox or online press room; it should be a resource for your target audience.

2   All posts should leave the reader with the impression that you spent a lot of time thinking about the post and how to 'wow' them. Blogs should be 400-600 words and should not be written like a newspaper article.

3   Stick to your goal of blogging whether it's weekly, bi-weekly or daily. As a rule of thumb, blog at a minimum of two times a month or don't blog at all.

4   Always have a photo to couple with the content. Try and mix it up with videos and slide shows. Offering contests/trivia on your conference centre blog is a sure way to generate excitement.

5   Follow blogging etiquette, leave insightful comments on other industry blogs and respond to comments on your blog; the bloggers that comment deserve a thank you and/or a response.

In her Hospitality Marketing blog for Cvent, *1-2-3 Easy Steps Toward a Great Social Strategy*, Dede Mulligan notes that comments made by members of the public on blogs and other social media can be negative as well as positive, and she emphasises that it is vital that negative comments in particular should be answered on a timely basis: 'I believe the sooner the better. If the comments are really negative, try and move the person off-line to a direct messaging forum or a telephone conversation. But by all means, NEVER remove negative comments'.

It seems inevitable that as more people choose to use the social media in their professional lives as well as their private lives, a growing number of venues will experiment with these tools. A clear indication of this trend can be found in the *ICCA 2012 Venue Trends Survey*, which showed that among the most popular job titles for new positions created in venues since 2009 were Social Media Manager and Digital Media Communications Manager.

Sustainability

Significantly, the other popular job title for new positions created by venues, as highlighted in the *ICCA 2012 Venue Trends Survey*, was that of Eco Manager. In that survey, in response to the question 'Has your venue adopted a sustainability programme?' 65% of the venues answered yes and 35% answered no. 61% said that they were actively marketing their sustainability programme.

Details of the type of initiatives taken by the venues as part of their sustainability programmes are shown in Figure 7.3.

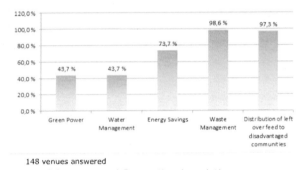

2012 Venue Trend Survey

Sustainability

What initiatives has your venue developed to reduce environmental impact?

148 venues answered

International Congress and Convention Association

Twitter: #ICCA12

Figure 7.3: Sustainability initiatives reported to the 2012 Venue Trend Survey. Source Dobler-Jerabek (2012)

7

The *Maritz Future of Meetings Survey* research discusses the 'Three Shades of Green' for venues: 'Be green, eat green and save green', noting that the challenge for meeting venues of the future will be how to do all three at the same time. In the findings of the research, the discussion of sustainability for venues typically focuses on the provision of locally grown food, organic food and healthier dietary options, with respondents making such comments as:

☐   'Green meetings are still growing in popularity'

☐   'I think venues need to follow trends in the market and stay flexible. For example, a hot trend is green meetings, green living, etc. If you can capitalize on the moment, it can give you a boost.'

But some survey respondents also express concern at the fact that 'green' initiatives are seldom cost-free: 'Green initiatives can be tricky based on the cost of organic and local food options as well as the extra steps in food composting/measurement etc.' 'It takes money to upgrade venues to meet green standards. For example, it can be challenging to find the capital for a new green roof.'

The authors of the Maritz survey conclude that the dilemma facing venues as they move forward is how to balance these conflicting ideas, and predicts that 'while the number of green meeting venues will grow, they will likely remain in the minority for the near future. With spiralling costs for food and sustainability initiatives on one side, and on the other, a demand for transparent sustainability practices, specifically local food products, increased food options (e.g., greater variety and healthier) along with lower costs; meetings venues are in a seemingly no-win situation ... While some venues will choose to specialise and cater to the green movement, others will concentrate on a more cost-driven customer base'.

In fact, there is a growing body of evidence that lower costs and a drive towards more sustainable practices in venues may not be incompatible. A participant at the IACC Thought Leader Summit 2012: Designing Meeting Experiences for Tomorrow, Bruce Burkhalter of Benchmark Hospitality International made a convincing case that sustainability need not be a cost to venues when he said, 'We have strong energy-efficiency plans and materials recycling programs, plus we recycle all our food waste. As a result, our total waste streams have gone down as much as 80 percent. To promote our overall value to clients, then, we have to get that message out better. After all, this issue has become very important not only to client organizations but to the next generation of meeting attendees.'

The crucial factor most likely to determine the extent to which venues adopt sustainability practices will be the level of demand for such features and how much venues can use green measures as a selling point. The jury appears to be still out on this question, which researchers Bauer and Lam raised over ten years ago, speculating that 'if the environmental performance of venues would become a key selection criterion for organisations' meeting planners and convention organisers, the management of venues would no doubt be very quick in changing their ways to cater for a more environmentally-friendly market'.

Encouragingly, of the venues polled for the *ICCA 2012 Venue Trends Survey*, 48% reported that their clients were requesting their sustainability programme.

In terms of getting the sustainability message over to clients, examples abound of venues that have distinguished themselves in the market through their endeavours in this area. On an international basis, one of the best-known is the Vancouver Convention Centre with its well-publicized green roof and active bee colonies (which produced 140 pounds of honey in 2010). The six-acre green roof supports 400,000 indigenous plants and grasses. It may well be in the near future that venues adopting the three shades of green will become the norm, rather than the exception.

However, it is worth remembering that closely linked with sustainability in the sense of 'green' meetings and venues, is the broader concept of Corporate Social Responsibility which also includes the notion of 'social legacy' – taking into account how an organisation's business activities impact upon the people who constitute the community where these activities take place. The case-study below describes the CSR and social legacy activities of the BT Convention Centre in Liverpool, UK.

BT Convention Centre, Liverpool: Corporate Social Responsibility Strategy

7

The BT Convention Centre is part of ACC Liverpool, which is also home to Echo Arena. Their detailed CSR strategy is described in the venue's statement below.

Through a series of focused and strategic CSR initiatives we intend to offer our employees, stakeholders and clients the optimum opportunity and support to conduct their business at ACC Liverpool in an ethical, sustainable and responsible manner.

In doing so, we aim to ensure that ACC Liverpool's business performance impacts in a positive way on our local communities, partners and stakeholders, as well as minimising the negative impact that our business may have on the natural and citywide environment.

BT Convention Centre and Echo Arena from the water.

Delegates at the annual ASDA staff conference, in the BT Convention Centre

Aims

The aim of developing a CSR Strategy is to ensure that ACC Liverpool continues to build upon its position as a responsible business for both its customers and its employees.

ACC Liverpool is committed to sustaining a well managed, profitable business that is ethical and responsible in terms of its impact on the environment, employment policy, and social and economic contributions to the local community. It is through the development and delivery of the CSR strategy that this position will be monitored and measured and through which further opportunities will be identified.

ACC Liverpool's CSR Objectives fall into five CSR Commitments

1. Committed to our Community
Through community investment, educational initiatives and employee volunteering, ACC Liverpool is committed to supporting the local community.

2. Respectful of the Environment
Through the development and delivery of sustainable initiatives, both linked to the building and infrastructure of ACC Liverpool and also to its employees, clients and customers, ACC Liverpool is committed to respecting its environment , reducing the impact its business has upon the local and general environment, as well as being an industry leader in sustainability.

3. Committed to Responsible Purchasing through the Supply Chain
Through our procurement and supplier management processes, ACC Liverpool is committed to always acting as a fair partner, both for suppliers and service partners.

4. Accountable in the Marketplace
We aim to extend this commitment to our clients where possible, to assist them with their own CSR objectives, facilitating their presence in our local community and allowing their events to have a lasting legacy in Liverpool through our support of the third sector.

5. Responsible in the Workplace
Through responsible Human Resource processes and policies and an aligned Internal Communications framework, ACC Liverpool is committed to diversity, inclusion, education, training, development and the promotion of health and wellbeing in the work place.

7

Achievements to date

Community

In August 2011, ACC Liverpool deployed more than 95 employees to help develop and transform a plot of land in Speke, south Liverpool. The open space was regenerated into an allotment which the Liverpool Food Alliance will now use to produce locally grown food for organisations such as the YMCA to benefit from.

Environment

ACC Liverpool hosted what is believed to be the UK's first carbon neutral business dinner on 14th March at the Global Entrepreneurship Congress. The entire event was carbon neutral, from the locally sourced ingredients being delivered by bicycle through to car sharing and 'green travel plans' developed for guests. The dinner will help raise awareness amongst business leaders of the complex challenges around managing food, water and energy consumption and how they interrelate.

Many of the portable ingredients were delivered by bicycle; delegates were encouraged to take public transport or car share and provided with a 'green travel plan'. The three course menu of local speciality dishes were prepared and cooked by Heathcotes, with help from Liverpool Community College students and all of the ingredients sourced from within a 50 mile radius of the venue. All event correspondence was electronic and the only paper materials used were on tables and handmade using recycled materials by Liverpool Community College Art Department. Heathcotes, the venue caterers, worked with suppliers to reduce packaging and waste.

Responsible Purchasing

We are committed to supporting local suppliers and in 2011 held our inaugural Supplier Innovation Day - an annual event where we actively engage with new and existing local suppliers to communicate our sustainable and CSR commitments and objectives and keep them informed of new initiatives and goals going forward.

Marketplace

In January 2012, we helped retailer Asda leave a lasting legacy in Liverpool following its annual staff meeting by donating food to hundreds of homeless people across Merseyside. The team at ACC Liverpool introduced Asda to the Liverpool branch of the YMCA to arrange the donation of non-perishable items to the YMCA which went on to support 262 homeless people across the region.

Workplace

85% of our workforce have been employed since we opened in 2008 and 93% of our workforce have been recruited from the Liverpool city region.

Our people are at the root of the venue's success and, as such, are engaged on a regular basis to support, promote and provide ideas for our sustainable activities.

Generational factors

Arguably, much of the 21st century impetus towards green meetings and use of technology at events, as described above, is being driven by the youngest generation of meetings planners and participants, Generation Y. Also known as Millennials and most frequently defined as those born between 1977 and 1995, this cohort represents the fastest-growing age group in the global workforce. It has been estimated that by the year 2020, 75% of the world's workforce will comprise members of Generation Y. This rapid growth in the numbers of this younger generation in professional employment will usher in an era of new expectations and demands for venues seeking to win business from Generation Y meetings planners and seeking to satisfy the needs of the growing body of Generation Y participants.

Their established profile as a generation makes them naturally disposed towards venues that can display their green credentials, as they appear to be far less tolerant of waste and the other negative impacts of large meetings and events on the natural environment. They also appear to care more about the human environment. Many commentators agree that Generation Y may constitute the most socially-conscious and civic-minded generation yet. For example, Cone's *2006 Millennial Cause Study* found that 68% of the Generation Y members surveyed would refuse to work for a company without a strong Corporate Social Responsibility track record. In fact, the study showed that 74% of the members of Generation Y will pay more attention in general to companies that do practice sound CSR policies.

With the passage of time, we will learn more about how the distinguishing characteristics of Generation Y will impact upon meetings venue design and the venue sales process. However, some insights can already be gleaned from a research project carried out in 2013, when the International Association of Conference Centres Emerging Trends Committee and Development Counsellors International (DCI) surveyed meeting planners of various generations. The objective was to establish whether there are generational preferences among meeting planners – and whether these preferences shape how meeting space is selected. For the purpose of this study, the generations were defined as Mature (age 66 and older), Baby Boomer (age 47-65), Generation X (age 33-46) and Generation Y/millennial (age 18-32).

Overall, it was found that the generations have very similar preferences. However, the survey highlighted a few differences which venue sales staff should keep in mind when selling to meeting planners of different generations:

- ☐ **Matures**: When pitching to a meeting planner of the mature generation, provide details on business-friendly guest rooms, spaces that are conducive to learning and collaboration as well as off-site activities that are within walking distance of the venue.

- ☐ **Baby Boomers and Generation X**: Promote the venue's Wi-Fi capabilities. Like Matures, these generations are also interested in spaces that are conducive to learning and collaboration. They are apt to decline a facility for inadequate meeting space (size/quality/layout) as well as cost and/or excess charges.

- ☐ **Generation Y**: The top two reasons that this generation is likely to decline a facility are the same as Baby Boomers: inadequate meeting space and cost/excess charges. However, Generation Y cares deeply about the appeal of the destination, so it is beneficial to provide them with information on entertainment and evening activities that are available off-site. In addition, this younger generation is interested in space that provides the ability to recognize key performers, so if a venue has excellent facilities for an awards banquet, these should be given prominence in any discussions with this generation.

Growing interest in unique venues

The technological and demographic trends outlined in this chapter, as well as the changing approaches to meetings design mean that demand for venues is likely to become more fragmented and diverse in the future. Many commentators believe that this development will give rise to greater use of niche locations, including non-traditional, unique or unusual venues. The *Maritz 2012 Future of Meeting Venues Survey* expresses the view that the rise in smaller meetings, as well as shorter meetings, is causing the market to increasingly consider the idea of booking non-traditional venues. Respondents confirmed this trends with comments such as:

☐ 'Smaller meetings will be the trend at casinos, parks, museums, and large restaurants.'

☐ 'Smaller meetings may begin meeting in less formalized settings... rather than hotels, etc., they may choose more remote, more relaxed environments.'

☐ 'Everyone wants something new, something fresh, something no one has ever seen.'

☐ 'Venues with a "plain" identity will start to suffer... the volume of meetings will decrease.'

☐ 'Meetings are looking for options other than cookie cutter type of venues.'

☐ 'Attendance increases at unique venues and delegates are more engaged, interested and therefore more apt to learn, gain from the experience.'

One aspect of the appeal of many unique venues is their 'sense of place' and individual personalities. In MPI's *Future of Meetings* report (2013), the architect Robert Hopkins made the following predictions: 'We see venues becoming more and more specific in terms of their time and place. We'll see fewer isolated and cookie-cutter institutions, and more venues that embrace their place—from design of space to décor. They'll 'go local' by featuring local materials, local foods, local artists, local icons and local talent'.

7

One agency already seeing evidence of this growth in popularity of unique venues is Grass Roots, the UK-based global provider of business improvement consultancy services. Grass Roots reported in its 2011 Meeting Industry Report that more than half the corporate meeting planners working with their meetings, events and communications division had selected a venue classified as 'unique' or unusual, the previous year. The growth of the unique venue sector has meant that Grass Roots has developed a special team for the sourcing of unusual venues so that their clients' briefs can be matched to the offerings of the latest and widest range of venues. Grass Roots' Head of Venue Innovation, Gemma Mock believes that to a buyer every unique venue offers something different and lots of flexibility: 'They create an unforgettable experience and offer greater creativity. Often they are a blank canvas that allows organisers to do what they want.'

Grass Roots works with a broad range of venues, both in the UK and internationally, but with unique venues Mock finds that she and her colleagues have to manage meeting planners' expectations carefully, especially with regard to what will be provided and the level of service they might expect. While conventional hotels have dedicated conference or event managers, many unusual venues do not because their primary function is normally something different, such as a restaurant, a museum, etc. 'We also have to educate the venues as to our role and how we operate, particularly in the area of safety and risk assessments and what our expectations are, together with those of our clients'.

What types of event are best suited to a unique venue? According to Grass Roots' Events and Communications Global Supply Chain Director, Alan Newton, the reality is that 'You don't know until you receive the brief from the client, although we tend to place bigger events into individual venues because they demand a unique experience with a big wow factor to impress internal or external stakeholders.' Gemma Mock adds: 'Clients tend to expect a hotel-standard of equipment to be available on-site at a unique venue, so any event at a unique venue needs a great deal of planning. We also need to be aware of the financial stability of the venue and highlight this to the client, and this is done through our RFP process.'

As more individual venues have entered the market, the need for venues to differentiate themselves has increased too. It is no longer enough just to be different; operators have to explain what makes their venues different. To achieve this, many venue operators are busy building brands. Alan Newton explains: 'Their products vary; many are non-residential, which reduces their appeal and limits their potential, although clever marketing can have a huge impact.' Brand fit – or alignment – is a growing trend in venue selection, as Newton confirms:

> More and more companies, particularly media and fashion houses, are very brand-led. They want to use venues that reflect or compliment their own brand values and definitely gravitate to unusual venues. Even if a hotel is being used it tends to be one of the more unconventional, quirky or boutique hotels. Even the more traditional corporates, such as professional services firms are now looking for venues that reflect that brand image and have moved away from conventional venues. However, that said, there are a plethora of hotels that have individuality within their venues, such as ornate or quirky banqueting rooms and facilities that could equally be classified as unique and unusual; they're just not that good at shouting about them.

Since it is that uniqueness and quirkiness that resonates with a growing number of their clients, venues with those qualities should make optimum use of them in the sales and marketing process in order to emphasise that their property can provide the wow factor, while still getting all the basics right.

This chapter has highlighted some of the key challenges facing venue sales staff as the market for their facilities and services continues to mutate at a rapid pace. The ideas and techniques described in this book will provide readers with the road-map they will need in order to respond to these – and other – transformations in the market environment.

In the midst of change, one constant imperative remains however: success in the meetings industry, as ever, will always be based on innovation, flexibility and an ability to be competitive in a highly contested market. Knowing and understanding clients' needs, and working in partnership with them to make their events successful will always help a venue to stand out from the crowd and prosper, even in the most challenging conditions.

7

Sources

Bauer T G and Lam L (2003) 'The greening of convention venues', in *Proceedings of 2003 Convention & Expo Summit*, Hong Kong Polytechnic University

CIC and HSMAI (2013) *Getting up to Speed: Event Bandwidth*, Convention Industry Council and Hospitality Sales and Marketing Association International

Cone (2007) *The 2006 Millennial Cause Study: The Millennial Generation: Pro-Social and Empowered to Change the World*, Cone Inc.

Davidson R (2011) Web 2.0 as a marketing tool for conference centres, *International Journal of Event and Festival Management*, **2** (2), 117-138

Dobler-Jerabek, Reate (2012) The 2012 Venue Trend Survey, presentation to the 51st ICCA Congress, available at: www.slideshare.net/ICCAWORLD/se103-renate-doblerjerabek

Duffy C and McEuan M B (2010) *The Future of Meetings: The Case for Face-to-Face*, Cornell University School of Hotel Adminstration

Grass Roots (2011) *Creating and using unusual venues*, Grass Roots Meeting Industry Report

IACC (2012) *A Guide to Social Media*, International Association of Conference Centres

IACC (2012) *Thought Leader Summit 2012: Designing Meeting Experiences for Tomorrow*, International Association of Conference Centres

IACC (2013) *Generational Preferences in Meeting Location Selection*, International Association of Conference Centres

ICCA (2012) *Venue Trends Survey*, International Congress and Convention Association

Kopytoff V G (2010) Wi-Fi Overload at High-Tech Meetings, *New York Times*, December 28

Maritz (2012) *The Future of Meeting Venues* White Paper. Maritz Research

MPI (2013) *Future of Meetings* report, Meeting Professionals International

Mulligan D (2012) Hospitality Marketing blog for Cvent, 1-2-3 Easy Steps Toward a Great Social Strategy

Segar A (2009) *Conferences That Work: Creating Events That People Love*, www.conferencesthatwork.com

Vining S (2011) *The Future of the Meetings Industry: Why Certain Conference Innovators Are Winning*, The National Conference Center

Online sources of further information

Annual reports on trends in the global meetings and events industry

Advito Industry Forecast.
www.advito.com

American Express Meetings & Events Global Meetings Forecast.
www.americanexpress.com

Carlson Wagonlit Travel Travel Price Forecast.
www.carlsonwagonlit.com

EIBTM TrendsWatch Report.
www.eibtm.com

Grass Roots Meetings Industry Report.
www.grassrootshbi.com

IBTM Meetings Industry Research Reports.
www.ibtmevents.com/home/Global-Research/

International Association of Conference Centres (IACC) Trends in the
    Conference Center Industry Report.
www.iacconline.org

International Association of Congress Centres (AIPC) Member Survey Report.
www.aipc.org

International Association of Professional Congress Organisers (IAPCO)
    Members' Survey. www.iapco.org

International Congress and Convention Association (ICCA) Venue Trend
    Survey.
www.iccaworld.com

Meeting Professionals International (MPI) Business Barometer.
www.mpiweb.org

7

Appendix: International associations of interest to venue sales professionals

International Association of Conference Centres (IACC)

www.iacconline.org

A global trade association representing conference centres hosting meetings, training courses and conferences with average delegate numbers of no more than 100 persons. IACC member conference centres focus on meetings and the majority of their revenues are derived from this. IACC has over 300 unique members in 17 countries who all conform to exacting standards.

IACC members offer clients a CMP delegate rate (Complete Meeting Package), which is comprehensive per delegate package including all meals, room hire and meeting room technology. The CMP package approach to pricing meetings is popular amongst Meeting Planners as it presents an easy to budget approach. IACC also stages annual conferences attended by global delegates and also features a Global Copper Skillet Chefs cook-off competition, where finalists from 7 countries compete for the title of Global Copper Skillet Champion.

International Association of Congress Centres (AIPC)

www.aipc.org

With representation from over 53 countries around the world, the AIPC is committed to encouraging and recognizing excellence and professionalism in convention centre management, while at the same time providing the tools to achieve such high standards through its research, educational and networking programs.

AIPC membership is reserved for those convention centre managers with an expressed interest in participating in the international meetings market and whose venues have the facilities and services required to host such events. AIPC offers its members the opportunity to engage with industry colleagues and take part in a global network of international convention and exhibition centre professionals. It provides a means for learning about and participating in the key issues and opportunities facing the industry, both today and into the future.

International Association of Venue Managers (IAVM)

www.iavm.org

The IAVM currently has over 3900 members worldwide. Founded in 1924 as the Auditorium Managers Association, IAVM is the world's largest professional association dedicated to issues relevant to the management of public assembly venues. Association members include venue managers from amphitheatres, arenas, auditoriums, convention centres/exhibit halls, performing arts venues, stadiums and university complexes. The IAVM provides superlative leadership, cutting-edge innovation, advanced education, supportive advocacy, opportunities for networking and connection between venue professionals around the world. In addition, the association is an acknowledged source for valuable public assembly related research, information, services, and life-safety issues worldwide. Membership is reserved for those who work at or are associated with a qualified public assembly venue, and are actively involved with the management, administration, or operation of the venue.

Historic Conference Centres of Europe (HCCE)

www.hcce.com

The HCCE is a marketing focused association, that promotes conference and convention centres in heritage buildings. Founded in October 1996, and with a current membership of 26 centres in 13 countries, it is the only international association of historic conference centres in the world. The main objective of HCCE is to increase international and national awareness of the facilities available in its historic conference venues. The members of this alliance strengthen their brand-name and expand their services to their regional, national, and international clients. HCCE membership is an endorsement of a unique historic property that is professionally managed with modern meeting facilities and the latest technology. Therefore strict membership criteria apply, including: the conference centre must be located in a unique, well maintained building that is at least 100 years old; the core activity must be the staging of conferences; a professional management and price structure must be present; the conference centre must be open for business all year round; and it must have one plenary hall to accommodate a minimum of 150 persons, plus 3 to 4 breakout (syndicate) rooms.

Convention Sales Professionals International (CSPI)

www.cspionline.org

CSPI, formerly the Association for Convention Sales and Marketing Executives that was established in 1991, is dedicated to fostering a spirit of collaborative success between convention centre sales professionals and their convention sales counterparts in regional destination marketing organizations. CSPI brings together the sales professionals in conventions centres and those in destination marketing organizations so that they can seamlessly serve their shared clients. CSPI achieves this important goal through year-round programmes and events that provide numerous opportunities for continuing education, member communications, and knowledge exchange between members through monthly member conference calls, professional networking and social interaction with centre and DMO peers.

The CSPI Seal of Approval recognises DMO and Convention Centre members who have achieved exemplary sales and service for all the destination's stakeholders and customers, while championing industry best practices by evaluating, training and promoting excellence in collaboration.

Meeting Professionals International (MPI)

www.mpiweb.org

One of the meeting and event industry's most vibrant global communities, MPI was founded in 1972 to help its members thrive by connecting them with knowledge and ideas, relationships, and marketplaces. MPI membership is comprised of more than 20,000 members belonging to 71 chapters and clubs worldwide.

Membership categories include those who plan and/or oversee the management of meetings for corporations, associations and government organisations. Venues may join in the Suppliers category of membership. Member benefits include access to: Chapter and Club events, for networking with local colleagues and potential clients, and continuing education; the MPI Community Directory, which enables members to find and connect with others across the globe; the Job Board, MPI's Career Connections job resource; Exclusive Research - various white papers and reports throughout the year to keep the membership up to date; Industry Certifications – the opportunity to obtain a certificate in Meeting Management, the most advanced learning recognition for the industry; Webinars with expert speakers and programs, that empower event professionals to take action on their big ideas.

International Congress and Convention Association (ICCA)

www.iccaworld.com

> Founded in 1963, ICCA comprises a membership that represents the main specialists in handling, transporting and accommodating international events. Venue members represent one of the five sector of ICCA membership. ICCA's network of over 950 suppliers to the international meetings industry spans the globe, with members in 88 countries. ICCA membership includes the following benefits: a cost-effective way of winning international association meetings business; access to a global networking platform representing all sectors of the meetings industry; a strong, custom-designed education programme for senior industry practitioners; access to valuable resources such as reports and statistical data.

7

Index